D0231660

SHOTGUN AND SHOOTER

SHOTGUN AND SHOOTER

By

G. L. CARLISLE and PERCY STANBURY

Photography by G. L. Carlisle

NEW REVISED EDITION

BARRIE & JENKINS
London Melbourne Sydney Auckland Johannesburg

Barrie & Jenkins Ltd

An imprint of the Hutchinson Publishing Group

3 Fitzroy Square, London W1P 6JD

Hutchinson Group (Australia) Pty Ltd
30–32 Cremorne Street, Richmond South, Victoria 3121
PO Box 151, Broadway, New South Wales 2007

Hutchinson Group (NZ) Ltd
32–34 View Road, PO Box 40–086, Glenfield, Auckland 10

Hutchinson Group (SA) (Pty) Ltd
PO Box 337, Bergvlei 2012, South Africa

First published 1970
Reprinted 1973, 1977, 1978
Revised edition 1981

Printed in Great Britain by The Anchor Press Ltd
and bound by Wm Brendon & Son Ltd
both of Tiptree, Essex

British Library Cataloguing in Publication Data
Carlisle, G. L.
    Shotgun and shooter. – Rev. ed.
    1. Fowling
    2. Shooting
    I. Title
    799.2′4   SK311
        ISBN 0 09 145050 0

CONTENTS

CONTENTS

LIST OF ILLUSTRATIONS

Note: Action pictures in shooting papers and magazines are often worth studying with a critical eye to detail outside the main caption. Examination of a shooter's feet, hands and head will give an indication of his style and the likelihood of the shot being successful. The student can also learn by recognising wrong technique in others and so correcting his own mistakes.

FOREWORD

by

THE VISCOUNT HAMBLEDEN

I HAVE known Percy Stanbury for a long time and I am delighted to be able to write a foreword to *Shotgun and Shooter*. Not only has he taught me virtually all there is to know about the art of shooting but he has also fascinated and amused me by his many experiences. The two authors have a considerable knowledge of all the facets of shooting and have emphasised, quite rightly in my opinion, the importance of both safety and good manners, which are so vital to this sport. I was especially interested in the chapter on wildfowling which has an attraction all its own, and I found my mouth watering at the hints on cooking at the end of the chapter.

G. L. Carlisle also took the photographs which, by their remarkable attention to detail and immense variation, are invaluable to anyone, beginner or otherwise, who loves shooting.

HAMBLEDEN

[13]

PREFACE
TO THE FIRST EDITION

THE object of this book is to describe some of the wider interests and pleasures associated with shotgun shooting apart from mere accuracy – to encourage and instruct the uninitiated and, it is hoped, to be of practical use even to the experienced sportsman. For more technical details, the reader is referred to *Shotgun Marksmanship* from which, for the purpose of clarity, some brief extract is given in this present book.

Amplification of some of the points mentioned in that book appear in this one in response to questions put to the authors either by readers or pupils. The stories in the book, which all point a moral, have not been invented; they are true. Although one volume cannot become a Complete Shooter, everything in it is of practical value. Most of the books listed in Appendix J ought to be in the library of the complete shooting man.

Throughout this book, the gun as a weapon is printed with a small 'g'. The man who shoots, when described as a 'Gun', has a capital 'G'.

The authors wish to thank all those kind friends who allowed themselves to be photographed, and also Imperial Metal Industries (Kynoch) Ltd., for advice about ammunition; the Proof Masters of the London and Birmingham Proof Houses, and the Gun Trade Association for permission to reprint in the appendices some of their notes on proof, second-hand guns, magnum cartridges and the law; and the Game Conservancy for help and advice.

[15]

PREFACE
TO THE REVISED EDITION

THIS new revised edition includes additional stories of the behaviour of shooting men and their dogs, each one exemplifying some facet of shooting experience. Hoping to avoid any charge of pontificating, we nevertheless feel confident that both novices and pundits may be moved to smile occasionally *and* appreciate that the tales do point lessons of practical value.

Prices throughout the book have been brought up to date, although continuing inflation will doubtless cause them to be further increased as the seasons go by.

SHOTGUN AND SHOOTER

CHAPTER ONE

INSTRUCTION

LEARNING about shooting covers a very big field of
activities. The most obvious one, of being able to shoot
straight, is best learned when young. Even so, experienced
sportsmen can still be taught, too – if they are willing.

Today's youngsters usually have less opportunity for
learning about shooting than did the boys of forty or fifty
years ago who could often, during school holidays, serve a
sort of amateur apprenticeship under a gamekeeper. In this
way, lads who were keen on shooting learned about the
countryside and natural history and woodcraft as they
learned how to handle a gun. The luckier ones had a strict
father who made sure that they had the rules of safety
dinned into them.

One might define three types of shooter, and this applies
to older men just as much as to boys: the chap who learns to
shoot straight but knows practically nothing about the
countryside and the birds and animals he wants to shoot;
the knowledgeable countryman who never bothers to learn
to shoot properly; and best of all, the sensible fellow who
gets the most out of his shooting by trying to learn as much
as possible about every aspect of it, from straight shooting to
keepering, natural history, dog training, wildfowling and so
on.

It is still possible, even in today's shrinking countryside,
to learn to be a complete shooter if the original approach is

correct and if sufficient trouble is taken. To begin with, it is *not* sensible for a young man to acquire a gun and then look for somewhere to use it; far better to find the shooting and then get a gun to suit the circumstances. An air rifle can make a satisfactory start for a boy, used under supervision on a range and then perhaps on the land of a friendly farmer. There is, however, a law about the use of all types of guns and rifles by young people under the age of seventeen (see Appendix E). It is most important that the first gun a boy gets his hands on is used to teach him safety, as well as how to shoot, and the elementary rule here is never to point the gun at anyone – not even if it is just a toy. The relaxation of this rule has caused many tragedies. (Plate 16.)

The adult who wants some shooting but does not have permission to enter suitable land should join a gun club which has some shooting rights and a liaison with local landowners, or join a shooting syndicate. For the youngster who is being initiated into shooting, however, a special care is required to start him on the right lines. It is a great advantage to start young, as with any sport, and it is tremendously helpful to learn correctly from the beginning, especially the elementary details of correct stance and gun mounting. This usually means, unless the boy is a 'natural', that he should be given his first lessons by a trained instructor and not by his father or a friend. Father may be a good and experienced shot but he is almost certain to tell his son something that is basically wrong or at least unsuitable. For instance, he will probably not even know whether the lad has a right master-eye or not; and he is unlikely to know much about the fit of his gun. When they do go to the shooting school, it is best if father keeps in the background as much as possible so that the boy does not become anxious when he misses the clays.

[20]

The father's role in instructing the young shot is to encourage him and show him how to enjoy the sport as a whole, explaining that it is pointless being miserable over missed shots, bad form to talk about successful shots and even worse to claim as one's own birds those that have been shot by someone else. The boy needs to be told beforehand what is likely to happen during the day; and afterwards, a kindly post-mortem can explain events and what went wrong and what went right, with a particular regard to safety rules – such as checking that the gun is unloaded at the end of the shoot.

A very small gun which can be used to coach the more precocious youngster who wants to start 'shooting flying' when he is about nine years old is the No. 3 Saloon gun. Sometimes called a Garden gun, it costs some £50 and the 9mm. cartridges are about £5 for fifty. One such lad, who was allowed to use a No. 3 to scare bullfinches away from an orchard during blossom time, found that he could get some excellent practice later in the summer by shooting wasps! He used to stand near the nest and take three going-away shots, followed by three incoming ones. Then he moved round to the side and tried the crossing shots. It worked very well and was a good apprenticeship before he moved up to a 20-bore a few years later.

Now we will visit a shooting school and examine some of the basic factors which contribute to straight shooting. Leaving for the moment the fitting of the gun and testing its pattern, which are discussed in Chapter Two, we go out on the ground for a lesson. The first advantage is that you are alone with the instructor. Nobody else is watching – least of all the other pupils, busy banging away on other parts of the shooting grounds. You will gain confidence as you do exactly what the instructor tells you. He can see the shot in the air

[21]

and correct your mistakes. You can be sure that he has had some really appalling pupils before you came along, and no degree of bad shooting surprises him any more. Instructors are asked some extraordinary questions by quite experienced shooters and given strange explanations of what they think they are doing wrong. For example : 'I can't think why I missed those last three clays. I shot *exactly* as I did before.' He didn't.

'I'm missing birds to the left because I get off balance. Why is that?' There are two reasons, but it's not just a question of balance.

Over the telephone : 'I'm shooting pretty well, but I need your help. Yesterday I missed a pheasant on my right, almost overhead. An easy shot, but I *missed*. What did I do wrong?' Sorry, you'll have to come to the school and show me.

The pupil is practically never doing what *he* thinks is wrong. The instructor will soon spot the real error and probably put it right in a few shots. Shooting, as far as the actual firing of the gun is concerned, is a very individual action and each pupil exhibits one bad habit or another. Equally, when he shoots straight, the pupil can be unaware of just what he did that brought success. If you ask a good shot how he does it, he will probably be unable to tell you; and if a friend asks how *you* managed to pull off some difficult shots, the kindest thing you can do is to tell him, as politely and modestly as possible, that you really do not know. But an experienced shooting coach *can* see what you are doing, all of it, from footwork to gun mounting, swing, trigger pulling and on to the pellets in the sky (Plate 15.)

The main principle of shotgun shooting is to keep the eye on the target and point with the left hand. A well-fitting gun then follows eye and arm, with the body pivoting in the required direction. The gun is scarcely seen by the shooter, just as you do not watch a hammer when you are hitting a nail with it.

When a bird is seen and accepted as coming into range, the gun must not be flung up to the shoulder and the barrels waved across the sky, chasing after the bird until the shooter decides he had better pull the trigger soon or his quarry will have departed out of range. But that is what often happens when the uninstructed novice first gets his hands on a shot-gun. Quite likely, he soon realises that the birds he is trying to shoot are moving fast, so he tries to quicken up his drill, whips the gun up, fires, and is more than a little sad to see that he has missed; although, in actual fact, he has hit what his gun aimed at, which was a piece of air a couple of yards behind his target. The correct procedure is to hold the gun with the butt down and the muzzles out in front, pointing up at about 45 degrees, and to move the left hand so as to keep the muzzles between the bird and your eyes. The muzzles are then held on the line of flight all the time while the gun is mounted, and the shot is taken as mounting is completed and the barrels come into line where your eyes are looking. (Plate 3.) Swinging the gun ahead of the bird, giving it forward allowance, or lead, will be explained later. At the moment, you should concentrate on handling your gun correctly and safely, and understanding how to place it in the correct position for shooting. We will examine the correct way to mount the gun from the beginning.

Good gun mounting requires a correct stance and grip and aim, and a stylish technique to co-ordinate all the movements. If you can master the several actions in correct mounting, you will be able to shoot reasonably well with any gun under any circumstances; but for top performance, a properly fitted gun is essential. A made-to-measure gun,

[23]

however, will not be of much help if the man behind it has not learned how to handle it.

The stance should be comfortable and, although it may vary a little according to the build of the shooter, the feet ought to be fairly close together. The general attitude is that of a half turn to the right front. Common faults are feet too far apart and the right foot nearly alongside the left, so that the shooter's chest is almost facing his target instead of being at an angle of about 45 degrees to the line of fire. Nearly all the weight is on the left foot; the right heel is just clear of the ground, and a slight forward lean induces a feeling of mild resistance in the left hip; it is not a tension, for the whole body from the hips up must be able to rotate right or left for slightly more than a right-angle without the feet being moved. The left knee is not bent, and it is the only joint that is kept stiff during the rotating movements.

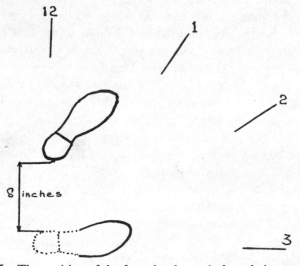

FIG. I – The position of the feet, the shooter's front being towards 12 o'clock.

This swinging from side to side is worth practising with the arms held out horizontally in front of you, palms facing down, keeping the left hand nearly opposite the right. It is more difficult when pivoting to the left, but that does not matter since, when shooting, the left arm is in front of the right as your chest remains obliquely to your front. Then practise pivoting while holding the gun. This ought to impress on you how you can get your body round to face the target, and that it is wrong to move your arm across your body and turn your head.

Balance should be perfect throughout these rotational movements and the gun-barrels must stay level, which they will do if body and shoulders remain square. But any swaying of the body will drop a shoulder. It is therefore not correct to shift the weight to the right foot and raise the left heel when swinging to the right, because this will cause the right shoulder to drop and so will cant the barrels sideways and make the shot miss low.

The gun should be gripped firmly with the right hand at the small of the butt, sometimes called 'grip' or 'hand' – a good solid hold which could raise the gun to the shoulder without using the left hand at all. The left hand has an entirely different sort of grip which varies from a loose hold, through which the gun can slide, to a firm grip between fingers and thumb but not using the palm of the hand to grasp the gun.

Before arranging the position of the left hand on the gun, consider the vital function of that hand in aiming the gun. Raise your left hand out in front of you and point at any object with the forefinger. There is an automatic co-ordination between eye and finger and both are concentrated on the same object. Now turn over the palm of your left hand and extend the thumb straight out and slightly to the left.

[25]

Your left hand and arm are now pretty well in the correct position for holding and pointing a game gun.

The left hand is always thrust out at your target. Its hold, initially, from wherever it was on the gun while you were at rest, is light and the barrels can slide through it. This hand moves first in mounting the gun and it puts the muzzles on the target and holds them there while the butt is down. Then, as the right hand brings up the butt to the shoulder and cheek, the barrels slide through the fingers of the left hand, which grips them when the butt is locked into the shoulder. The attitude of the left hand is with the thumb lying straight along the left barrel, the first finger running up between and underneath the two barrels, pointing, and the three remaining fingers gripping the right barrel along its side. There should be no finger or thumb over the top of either barrel and no weight in the palm of the hand.

If the thumb comes over the left barrel, your line of sight – instead of running straight up the centre of the barrels over the rib – will be deflected up the right barrel, which means that the barrels are sighted slightly to the right and you will miss on that side. Should the fingers appear over the right barrel, the converse applies and the shot misses to the left. This description of the left hand lying under the barrels with the forefinger extended applies to the normal double-barrelled game gun.

Beginners nearly always hold a gun with the left hand too far back. If they also adopt a tight grip and have fingers or thumb on top of the barrels, they tend to try to look over the top. Sighting thus becomes wildly erratic. There is no specific position along the barrels where the left hand must be positioned, but a straight or very nearly straight arm is recommended. It gives better balance for the gun, keeps the muzzles up and is the natural position for pointing. The

[26]

closer grip with a bent left elbow is usually adopted where the shooter has graduated to the shotgun from the rifle and thinks in terms of a tight hold and aiming instead of a freely moving left arm and pointing.

On a standard game gun, the fore-end contains the ejector mechanism and holds the gun together. Its location is not fixed with the primary object of accommodating the owner's left hand. His hand might fit comfortably over the fore-end but more likely part of it, at least, reaches conveniently in front, on the metal of the barrels.

Anyone familiar with the delightful writings of Richard Jefferies (*The Gamekeeper at Home*, *The Amateur Poacher*, etc., written around 1880) – and no countryman should be *un*familiar with such works – may remember the stories of the boy called Bevis. In one of these, an American sharp-shooter breaks innumerable glass balls thrown up into the air, using a ·22 rifle. When the family get home after the show there is much discussion on how the shooting was done.

'I know how he did it!' exclaims Bevis. 'The secret is in this,' and he holds out his left arm. Jefferies goes on to explain the importance of the long left arm for snap shooting with a rifle and its application to shotgun shooting: 'The left hand is thrust out, and, as it were, put on the game. Educate the left arm; teach it to correspond instantaneously with the direction of the glance . . . let the mind act through the left wrist. The left hand aims.'

This is admirable, except that the verb 'aim' is better avoided because of its association with the careful sighting along the barrel of a rifle. The shotgun user should rather think in terms of 'pointing'. Not everyone finds it comfortable to shoot with a straight left arm, but many first-class shots do so. It is certainly a good drill for a learner to acquire before he picks up less helpful habits.

With your stance correct and a knowledge of how to grip the gun you will need to practise mounting, which calls for co-ordination of eye and brain with movements of arms and body – and, perhaps, feet as well. Mounting starts when the bird is first seen. The correct stance is taken, with the left foot pointing at about 1 o'clock from the target; the left hand pushes out the barrels towards the bird so that you can watch it over the muzzles; and as the bird swings to either side of you, your body pivots and allows the muzzles to stay on. At this stage, the stock is lying *along the lower forearm*, not down by your right thigh, with the butt by your elbow. (Plates 4, 5, 6, 7.) As the right hand then brings up the butt, the left arm thrusts out, gripping the barrels, and for a fraction of a second the gun is at eye level and the butt is just touching the shoulder but not bedded firmly against it. At this critical moment, your shoulder comes forward to meet the butt. As the butt comes hard into the shoulder, you squeeze the trigger. During the whole movement your body is pivoting as required by the movement of the bird, and your gun muzzles are swinging with it and being raised by the left hand to keep them on target.

The mounting of the gun is a deliberate, smooth and comparatively slow movement, and the body is relaxed until the instant of firing. As the gun meets the shoulder, the left arm is pulling it forward and this, combined with the tight grip of the right hand and the thrust forward of the shoulder, results in practically no recoil being felt. The cheek must be bedded closely on the stock and the head held normally erect – not bent down to get the eye low, nor bent back in instinctive fear of the shock of discharge. As the gun is fired, the left knee is stiff and the shoulder and neck muscles are tensed; but the hips remain fluid and continue the swing of

[28]

body and gun-barrels. Both elbows should be in a natural midway position, not pointing down to the ground and not stuck out horizontally. Common mistakes with beginners are to relax the grip at the moment of firing, to draw away the head or shoulder, and to flinch – all of which, besides ensuring a miss, result in the recoil giving them a blow on the shoulder or even on the upper biceps when the butt has slipped. Sometimes a smack in the mouth from the top of the stock can also be caused in this way. Have no fear when you fire a gun. Hold it firmly, be determined to master it, and have confidence that you are going to point it in the right direction and pull the trigger exactly when you want to.

One talks of mounting a gun slowly, but it is really the deliberation that needs emphasising. If you watch a good shot in action, he appears to be slow because he is precise and his movements are not hasty and jerked. Your mounting must also be slow but it must finish with a snap. You are leaning forward a bit as you mount the gun; you keep your eye unwaveringly on the target. But when your gun is up, you fire at once, with no dawdling about waving your gun across the sky in pursuit of your bird. If you see a shooter hanging in the aim like that, with his gun muzzles following a bird, you can be practically certain he is going to miss. It is very bad style; and even if its followers sometimes score a hit, they really scarcely deserve to.

Fundamentally, then, the sequence of gun mounting is:
1. Eye picks up bird, and body pivots with it.
2. Left hand puts muzzle on, butt still down.
3. Right hand brings up butt slowly, while body and left hand keep muzzle on line of flight.
4. Shoulder comes in to butt, and gun is fired.

When should you put the safety-catch to the firing posi-

[29]

tion? Basically, the answer is 'Only just before the trigger is pulled'. You should certainly *not* have the safety-catch off while you are waiting for birds, to appear. The correct time to push forward the safety-slide is as you prepare for your shot, and this means that three things happen simultaneously:

1. Weight on the left foot in the direction of the bird.
2. Muzzle in line with the bird, stock still down along the forearm.
3. Safety-slide pushed forward.

You then carry on mounting the gun and take the shot. But if for any reason you do not shoot, your immediate reaction as you lower the gun must be to push the slide back to 'Safe'. While you are in the ready position and pushing the safety-catch off, it is most important that your right forefinger should be along the trigger guard. It must not move on to the trigger until the next stage, when you bring the butt to your shoulder. If you allow your finger to stray on to the trigger too soon, there is every possibility that the action of pushing off the safety-catch with your thumb will result in a corresponding movement back of your finger, and the gun will go off. Besides being potentially dangerous to others, this can result in the top lever jabbing back on recoil and cutting the top of your thumb. To avoid risk of this injury the thumb should be trained to flick back to the side of the grip immediately it has operated the safety-catch.

It is sometimes advocated that the safety-catch should be pushed off as the gun is mounted, but this can be dangerous because the thumb may again be caught by the top lever if the gun is fired a little too quickly. It is better to flick off the safety-catch as you prepare for the shot.

Some specific points in mounting and firing the gun need emphasising in a little more detail:

[30]

Keeping the head up

The head should be held in a natural position for all shots. Although it has to be bent back a little for overhead shots, any movement to look to either side should come from a body pivot; the neck should not be twisted sideways. The head must not be lowered on to the stock. If you look at an object and then raise your right arm to point your finger at it and, at the same time, lower your head so that your chin touches your shoulder, you will find that when you raise your head to a natural position again your finger is not pointing at the mark; it is below it. A similar error occurs if you drop your head on to a gun-stock: The head must be 'locked' in a normal attitude. (Plates 8, 9, 10, 11.)

First aim

First aim with a gun is correct, although we should really call it 'point', just as when you quickly point your finger at something your eye ensures that your finger points true. If the gun fits and you are properly balanced, it will point where you are looking and no adjustment is necessary. It is useful to go outside – even quite a small garden will suffice – and practise mounting your gun at various marks around you to convince yourself of the trueness of first aim.

'Reading' your bird

This means watching the course of the bird carefully, putting the gun muzzles on to it and swinging through from tail to head. It does *not* mean raising the gun straight *at* the bird and firing. This fault often occurs with a bird approaching on the left, especially if the shooter is waiting with his gun-barrels pointing across his body to the left instead of to

[31]

the front. Then there is a tendency to 'take a short cut' and poke the gun at the bird instead of collecting it from behind and swinging through. (Plates 12, 13, 14.) 'Reading' also means appreciating whether a bird is rising or falling; a wing-flapping pheasant, as distinct from a gliding one, for instance, is nearly always rising, and on a crossing shot the gun should sweep, not through the bird, but along its back in order to keep the shot up.

Cheek on stock

The stock is held tightly on to the fleshy part of the cheek: not the cheek-bone or the chin-bone, but in between. And the cheek must stay there for an appreciable moment after the shot. A common cause of missing is raising the cheek too soon to watch the bird fall – only usually it doesn't! (Plate 21.)

The second barrel

If you miss with the first barrel, keep the butt to your shoulder, swing on and fire the second barrel. If you kill with the first barrel and want to use the second barrel for another bird, lower the butt a few inches off the shoulder, put the muzzles on to the second bird, 'read' it and mount the gun again to fire. (Plates 23, 24, 25.)

Forward allowance

This is a vexed question which has aroused countless arguments and theories. Briefly, one must shoot with a swinging gun and *keep the swing going* after pulling the trigger, so as to throw the shot in front of the bird's position at the instant

[32]

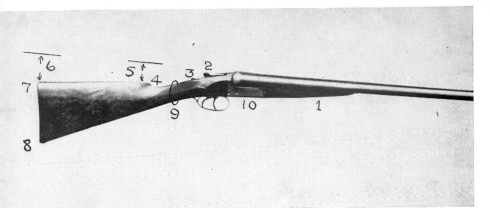

THE PARTS OF A SHOTGUN

1. Fore-end. 2. Top lever. 3. Safety catch. 4. Comb. 5. Bend, or drop, at comb. 6. Bend, or drop, at heel. 7. Heel, or bump, of butt. 8. Toe of butt. 9 Small of the butt, or grip, or hand. 10. Lock.
The gun is a 12-bore, box-lock, hammerless ejector. The ends of the barrels are not shown.

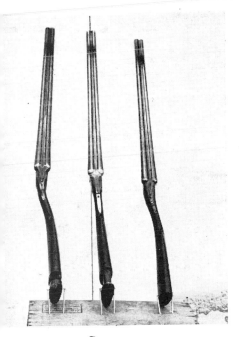

CAST-OFF
In the centre is a try-gun set with a good al of cast-off; the vertical black line shows w the stock has been moved to the right of e line of the barrels. On the left is an across-ed stock. On the right is a gun with nsiderable cast-off to align the barrels ntrally, between the shooter's eyes; this is a central-vision stock.

THE EYE OVER THE MUZZLES
3. The shooter places his gun muzzles exactly between his eye and the bird. Note stock well up by right forearm.

Incorrect Preparation for the Shot

4. He has some idea of lining up the muzzles between his eye and the bird but the stock is too low, almost at hip level.

Gun Muzzles off the Target

5. When he raises the butt from as far down as in Plate 4 the muzzles tend to drop, pivoting on his left hand. The barrels point below the line from eye to bird.

Correct Preparation for the Shot

6. The butt is well up along his forearm.

On Target

7. The small movement of the gun from its position in Plate 6 keeps the muzzles on. He kills his bird.

MOVING THE HEAD WITHOUT THE GUN

8. He is looking at a bird to the left but he has not brought the gun round as well. This is wrong.

EYE, BODY AND GUN BARRELS

9. He has pivoted his body to the left and brought the gun round too; the muzzles are in a line from eye to bird. This is correct, even though he is not yet sure whether he is actually going to take the shot.

TAKING THE SHOT

10. The bird has come in range, and the gun is right on it. Good style.

LOWERING THE HEAD

11. Bad style. He has dropped his head to the stock instead of looking up in a natural manner, and bringing the butt to his shoulder and the comb to his cheek. The shot will probably miss.

TAKING A SHORT CUT

12. This is wrong. He is looking up and to his left but he has left the gun behind. It is the incorrect way of watching a bird.

SHOOTING AT THE BIRD AND MISSING

13. He brings his gun straight up from the position in Plate 12 and shoots directly *at* the bird. No swing, no follow through, not much hope.

READING A BIRD

14. This is how he should have been in Plate 12, collecting the bird over the muzzles, ready to swing through it as the gun is mounted.

A SHOT AT PARTRIDGES

15. A successful shot at a covey of partridges by a good shooter. A shooting coach would note his ability, but also some faults

BOYS' DAY ON THE PHEASANT SHOOT

16. A boy may legally use a shotgun only when supervised by an adult. Here a youngster is enjoying his first experience of driven pheasants.

SWINGING THROUGH AND GIVING LEAD

17. Swinging through a low grouse; the bird was shot an instant later. The shooter leading it by about 4 feet, though he may well think he is giving no lead at all.

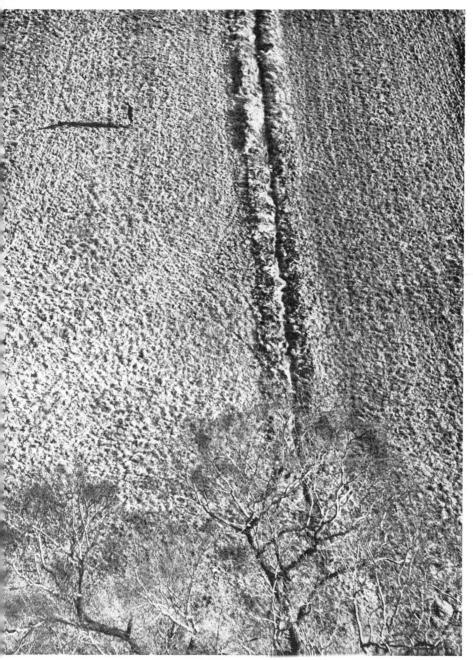

BIRD'S EYE VIEW

From the top of the 40-yards-high tower at a shooting school. Man with a gun in the left-hand corner. Targets at this height need an appreciable forward allowance. The es at the bottom of the picture are about 45 feet high, quite tall for a pheasant covert. ds flying just above the trees would be only about 20 or 25 yards above the Gun. To birds 40 yards up requires practice and experience to judge what the "picture" looks like.

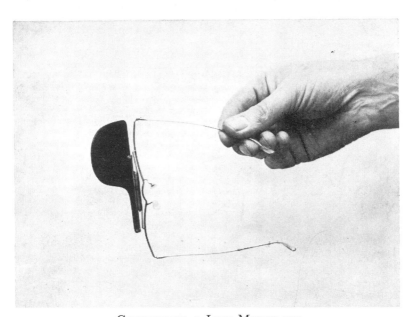

CONTROLLING A LEFT MASTER-EYE

19. A spectacle frame fitted with an opaque piece of plastic which can swivel to block vision from one eye, or enable both eyes to be used.

20. The special frame with the attachment blocking the line of sight of the left eye up along the barrels, while still allowing the wearer to use both eyes for looking downwards.

of firing. At long ranges the apparent speed of a crossing bird is less than at short ranges, and this slows down the speed of the swing. Something must be done to counteract this and so we give a forward allowance, or lead, in front of the bird. It is not a distance measured in feet but a 'picture' in the shooter's eye which, by experience, he knows is necessary for those particular circumstances. The picture varies enormously: some people speak of leading a high pheasant by 'a field gate', meaning ten feet or so; others claim that they do not lead their birds but 'shoot at his beak'. As any shooting coach knows, practically every normal shooter simply is not aware of *what* he really does; but if he remembers his 'picture' and kills his birds it does not matter.

Some quotes on the subject are :

'I have never shot in front of a bird.'

'For those clays from the high tower at the shooting school I reckon you need about ten feet forward allowance.'

'I seldom miss, I always aim six inches ahead of my target.'

'I led that duck about the width of my gun barrels.'

'There are some really high pheasants on that shoot. I got one or two with a lead of about eighteen feet !'

If you are learning to shoot, or trying to improve, go to a shooting school and have some shots at high clays, 40 yards up. (Plate 18.) When you miss, you can then experiment by giving them more lead, even an 'impossible' amount, until you hit them. When shooting live game, always look at the bird's head; do not be distracted by a cock pheasant's long tail. The picture that you work out as being the required forward allowance for various crossing shots depends on your own natural speed of swing and on your reaction time in assessing a target, deciding to shoot and pulling the trigger.

[33]

The one thing you must not do is to stop the swing as you fire: a 40 m.p.h. pheasant travels 6 feet in 1/10 of a second, and so only a very small check is needed to make the shot miss behind. If you follow through with your swing, you should be able to prevent any check. Good shots who claim that they give no lead do, in fact – because after the mental order to fire at the bird, the lead is unconsciously given on the overthrow of the gun.

An added difficulty about longer range shots is the mental persuasion that is needed to make one 'shoot into space' ahead of the bird, because the natural reaction is to shoot at least fairly close to it. But unless you are already a first-class shot who regularly kills them in beautiful style, without really knowing how, you should try to cultivate a picture which includes a forward allowance. (Plate 17.)

Style

Good style hits the target. When you miss, it is nearly always a fault in style. Practise gun mounting and pivoting the body from a correct stance. If you suffer any discomfort on a shooting day, such as a bruised shoulder, it is a sign of poor style – assuming, of course, that you have done first things first and had the gun properly fitted. If you have a bad style but still manage to hit a good deal of what you aim at, you may well decide to leave things as they are. The instructor can only say: 'If you really want to shoot better, I can teach you. But in sacrificing your old style, you will be worse at first. If you persevere, you will improve considerably.'

The eye over the muzzles

In preparing for a shot, at the beginning of gun mounting,

you have been told to put the muzzles on the bird so that they are in the line from your eye to the bird. More than that, you should always move the muzzles at the same time as the eye when you look at a bird which is likely to come in range. Do not look at the bird and leave the muzzles behind, as it were; because then, if you do decide to shoot as the bird passes to one side or the other, there is every likelihood that you will put up the gun without having 'read' the bird and poke *at* it instead of swinging through it. (Plates 12, 13, 14.)

As an example of the odd experiences of a shooting coach, a client once asked for a lesson, saying that his problem was that he often missed the simple going-away bird. He had some shots at clays and missed the first six, as the coach could see, by a couple of feet to the left. He was mounting his gun quite nicely and so the instructor suggested that he tried closing his left eye. The pupil looked a bit suprised but did what he was told and broke four clays in a row. He was delighted, and the instructor told him that perhaps his left eye was a little stronger and tended to take control on certain shots. 'That's what makes it all the more remarkable,' said the client. 'Because my left eye is a glass one!'

CHAPTER TWO

GUNS AND CARTRIDGES

Two Americans were on their way to shoot grouse in Scotland. On August 10th they called at a shooting school in southern England for some practice. One of them had a pair of guns bought in New York just before he left. He asked to go straight to the grouse butts to try his guns, but he could not hit a thing with them. The instructor saw that the shot was missing the clays by feet, to the left, and he said: 'Excuse me, sir, but I think you must be left-eyed.'

'What d'you mean? There's nothing wrong with my right eye!'

Patiently, the instructor explained about the 'master-eye' which takes control when both eyes are open, and tests soon showed that his client was so aggressively left-eyed that an across-eyed stock was needed. The client could not wink or even dim his left eye – and he wanted to keep it open, anyway, because it was his better eye. (Plate 61.)

'Then get me one,' said the American. 'I'll pay whatever it costs, but I must have it by tomorrow morning when I go to Scotland.'

The school telephoned several London gunmakers and by a remarkable stroke of luck one of them had a gun with an across-eyed stock, which was sent out, tested and delivered to its new owner just in time.

The second American had a very nice 20-bore and he shot well with it. Apparently, he normally fired only a few shots at a time; and when he started some concentrated shooting at the clay 'grouse', the gun became hot and jammed. Nothing would move. It was quite useless.

'When did you last have this gun examined by a gun-maker?' asked the instructor.

'Oh, I don't know. Not sure that I ever have. But I always clean it after a hunting trip.'

The gun was stripped there and then and found to be clogged up with thick old oil. When it had been cleaned and reassembled it worked perfectly.

Here are examples of two sportsmen keen enough to spend a good deal of money on their shooting but unaware of some vital requirements in their guns. Had they not visited the school and received some expert assistance, their grouse-shooting trip would have been ruined. It definitely pays to know something about guns and their limitations and char-acteristics, and to be aware of one's own, and not to suffer under the handicap of an unsuitable weapon.

Although there are several different bore sizes for shot-guns, the most popular is the 12-bore, more correctly termed 'gauge'. A fairly 'standard' game gun might have 28-inch barrels, weigh about 6½ lbs. and be a hammerless ejector, with either a boxlock or a sidelock. It would fire 2½-inch cartridges loaded with 1$\frac{1}{16}$ oz. of shot, and have an effective range of 40 yards at normal game. Unfortunately, as soon as we have listed these vital statistics, a host of desirable variations will occur to any experienced shooter, because a 'suitable' gun can only be so for its owner and the type of shooting he expects to find. We had better examine, briefly, some of these details of a game gun.

Short barrels, 25-inch, are claimed by their users to be quicker on the target and lighter: useful for driven partridges or skeet clay-pigeon shooting. Cheaper versions of such guns

[37]

are often poorly balanced, but the upward flip of the short barrels makes them tend to shoot high, which is desirable. Longer barrels, 30-inch, are steadier and reduce muzzle blast. Bigger cartridges with a bigger shot-load are required for longer ranges and for tougher birds such as geese; and then you need a heavier gun to absorb the greater recoil. And so it goes on. But for the moment, let us consider how to find a suitable and reasonably normal game gun.

Buy the best you can afford. At the top of the list an English best gun costs, in 1981, some £10,000 and delivery time is about two and a half years. Second-hand best guns appear in London sales-rooms and well-preserved ones, of perhaps forty years old, go for about £4000. A good new English boxlock gun costs about £2000 and second-hand ones can be found for about £500–£800. You can buy a new English-made single-barrelled 12-bore for about £150. Foreign guns can be good and they are often attractively priced; but some of them are very poor. They should never be bought except through a reputable retailer who is a member of the Gun Trade Association.

In buying second-hand it is better to avoid hammer guns, which are dangerous because of the necessity of lowering the hammer in order to uncock them; if the fingers slip off the hammers the gun will probably be discharged accidentally. A hammerless boxlock ejector is the most likely choice. A 'non-ejector' does, in fact, eject the cartridges a quarter of an inch or so when it is opened, but then the cartridges must be extracted by hand. An ejector has a spring which flicks them out. The boxlock, sometimes called 'Anson and Deeley' after its inventors, is simple and robust and unlikely to give trouble (Fig II). Sidelocks are more beautiful and more sophisticated; they are on detachable plates let into the side of the action and the best ones have intercepting sears which

[38]

THE LIMITATION OF THE SAFETY CATCH

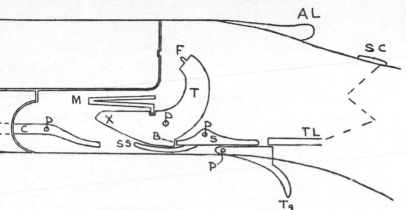

FIG. II. – *Explanation of the main parts of a Box Lock*

C   – Cocking Lever. Its rear end pushes up the end of the Tumbler marked X when the gun is opened and the barrels drop down.
M   – Mainspring. Here under stress, pushing against the Tumbler.
F   – Firing pin, or Striker, which strikes the cap on the cartridge.
T   – Tumbler, which is in fact the hammer.
B   – Bent, bearing against the nose of the Sear.
SS   – Sear Spring. Trying to push the front end of the Sear, its nose, upwards.
S   – Sear, in contact with the upper part, the blade, of the Trigger.
P   – Pivots, round which can move the Cocking Lever, Tumbler, Sear and Trigger.
Tg   – Trigger.
TL   – Trigger Lock. Actuated by the Action Lever in an 'Automatic Safety' lock, it slides forward and prevents the Trigger blade from being raised, and so locks the Trigger.
AL   – Action Lever. Opens the gun. Called a top lever when it is on top of the gun, its most usual position.
SC   – Safety Catch. When moved forward it brings the Trigger Lock back, free of the Trigger blade. The actual mechanism is not shown.

Note that in a double-barrelled gun most of these parts are repeated.

Method of Firing

1. The gun is now cocked and the Safety Catch is on.
2. Moving the Safety Catch forward slides the Trigger Lock back.
3. Pressing the Trigger pushes up the back end of the Sear.
4. The Sear nose at the front then dips down and slips off the Bent of the Tumbler.
5. The Mainspring exerts pressure on the Tumbler which pivots, so that the Firing pin jumps forward into the hole in the breech and fires the cartridge.

[39]

N.B. The Safety Catch only locks the Trigger, and in a worn gun the pressure of the Mainspring can be sufficient to push the Bent off the nose of the Sear, particularly if the gun is jarred; the Tumbler is then free to pivot round and fire the cartridge.

prevent the lock operating if the gun is jarred by, for instance, being dropped or falling over. The safety catch on most guns *only* prevents the triggers from being pulled. Sidelocks are more sensitive to fine adjustment of trigger pulls, but they are expensive. A good, normal boxlock is better than a cheap sidelock.

All guns must be proved and bear proof marks before they may be sold. 'Proving' a gun involves firing a special charge which sets up a higher pressure than that to which it would normally be subjected. The presence of proof marks is no guarantee that an old gun is still 'in proof'. The Gun Barrel Proof Acts of 1868 and 1950 forbid anyone to sell a gun which is not 'in proof' (see Appendix A).

If you are buying a second-hand gun, the seller may be a gun dealer or a private person. In the latter case, it would be advisable to send the gun to the Proof House for testing before you part with any money. There are also a few simple details you can examine. Take the fore-end off, hold the gun by the grip on its side and waggle it up and down; or hold the gun by its barrels and jar the butt gently. In either case, a worn action will be revealed by a rattle or a movement in it. Hold the gun up against the light and look for any slight gap between the breech and the face of the action; this should be a tight fit. Take the barrels off and suspend them with your finger under the lumps; tap them against a table edge and they should ring clear. If they do not, you can suspect loose ribs or even cracked barrels. Examine the barrels for dents on the outside and for pitting inside. But beware of 'lapped' barrels. Lapping means boring out the gun to remove the pitting, like reboring the cylinders of a car, and it can render the gun out of proof. It can be detected only by accurately measuring the bore. Hence the need to have a gun which is offered by a private individual checked by a proper gunsmith. The general appearance of the butt will give an indication of the amount of care the gun is likely to have received, and if the chequering is well worn it indicates that the gun has had a good deal of use.

For simplicity we are considering basically our standard game gun, as in Plate 1, but mention must be made of some of the variations available. Larger bores than 12- are used by wildfowlers, particularly for geese, but they are rarely made now and their cartridges are difficult to obtain. The term 'bore' refers to the number of lead balls of the same diameter as the gun's barrel which together weigh 1 lb. Thus a 10-bore is bigger than a 12-, an 8- is even bigger, and a 4-bore bigger still. Smaller guns are 16-, 20- and 28-bore, and the 'four-ten' which, paradoxically, is measured in inches. ·410 inches is its bore, and it is handy for a small boy learning to shoot rats and squirrels and rabbits. Do not imagine that the smaller bores are cheaper guns. Quite often, a 16- or 20-bore costs more than a 12-bore in similar condition because it has a rarity value.

Here are some more variations from standard:

Single-trigger

One trigger fires each barrel in turn. Contrary to general belief, a single trigger does not permit faster shooting than two triggers. Probably its only advantage is that it is easier to operate when wearing gloves. But single-triggers are expensive and liable to fail unless regularly maintained by a gunsmith.

Pistol grip

A half-pistol grip may be used on a single-trigger gun,

[41]

but there is no point in having one on a double-trigger gun. A straight hand stock is better, as it allows the finger to reach the second trigger more easily. A full-pistol grip has no advantage except, possibly, for a user who has some deformity of the hand.

Raised rib

Guns for clay pigeon shooting often have the rib raised and serrated, or 'file cut', to prevent light reflecting on it. The rib may also have ventilation holes for cooling. These modifications can be a help for some clay shooting – when the shooter aims his gun before the target is released – but they are not necessary for game shooting.

Enlarged fore-end

The recommended position of the left hand is under the barrels beyond the fore-end. In mounting his gun, the game shooter lets the barrels slide through his fingers and only grips with his left hand as he takes his shot. But the clay pigeon shooter grasps his gun firmly while he is waiting for the clay to be released, and so he often likes to have a longer fore-end designed to be held in his left hand. One such type of fore-end is called a 'beaver-tail' because of its similarity to the flattened round tail of a beaver.

Non-automatic safety

The action of opening a normal shotgun cocks it and also applies the safety-catch. On some guns, however – particularly the cheaper ones – the safety-catch is *not* operated and therefore must be applied by hand. This is a potentially dangerous feature of guns without automatic safety.

[42]

Over-and-under

One barrel is on top of the other, instead of the two being side by side. These guns tend to be more expensive and heavier than the conventional side-by-side gun. They are not quite so easy to load. But they are popular with clay pigeon shooters, who like the single top barrel along which to aim, particularly for trap shooting.

Self-opening guns

Many shooting men are unaware that such guns exist, and possibly some owners do not realise that less favoured mortals have to make do with standard guns. The true 'self-opener' drops its barrels, through the assertion of its main spring or an auxiliary spring, when the top lever is moved across, irrespective of whether the gun has been fired or not. It is a top price, Rolls-Royce, best gun for 'top people' who have opportunities of using its advantage of being quicker to reload when driven birds are streaming over. (Plate 34.)

Repeaters

These guns have one barrel and a magazine from which cartridges are reloaded by sliding back and forward the fore-end, as in the 'pump gun', or by using the movement of the recoil, or by diverting part of the propellant charge. They tend to be reasonably inexpensive but they are usually poorly balanced. They require a good deal of experience to hold steady for a quickly taken second shot and they are often not popular with other shooters. This is partly because, rightly or wrongly, repeaters are regarded as 'unsporting' and also because the barrels cannot be dropped to show one's friends that the gun is unloaded. Dropping the barrels of a normal shotgun also allows its user to check that they are free from any obstruction, such as snow or mud.

[43]

The working parts of automatics need to be kept scrupulously clean and this is often difficult for a mud-covered wildfowler.

Single-barrel guns

A one-shot single-barrelled shotgun is no bad choice for a young man with not much money to spend. They are cheap; the English ones are well made; and for the sort of rough shooting that their owners are likely to enjoy, the limitation of only one barrel will probably save cartridges. The real object of two barrels in a shotgun is to kill two birds without reloading – not to have a second shot at a bird missed with the first barrel!

Chromium-plating

Some guns, particularly those made abroad, have the inside of their barrels coated with an electro-plated deposit of chromium. This is supposed to offer resistance to wear and to produce better patterns, but these claims have not been substantiated. Disadvantages of chromed barrels are that the process may make the barrel steel more brittle, that repairs such as raising dents become infinitely more difficult and costly, and chromed barrels on old guns may conceal unknown amounts of wear or pitting. [Note Appendix A, 3 (c) (ii).]

Choke

This is a constriction at the end of the barrels which squeezes together the shot charge in order to improve its pattern. A barrel without choke is referred to as 'true cylinder' and the smallest amount of choke is called 'improved cylinder'; larger amounts are $\frac{1}{4}$, $\frac{1}{2}$, $\frac{3}{4}$ or full choke. A standard game gun usually has improved cylinder in the right barrel and $\frac{1}{2}$ or $\frac{3}{4}$ choke in the left. Quite often, foreign-made guns – particularly single-barrelled ones – are offered with full choke. The tight pattern of shot from such guns increases the difficulty of hitting a target at short ranges of fifteen or twenty yards, but it is a comparatively easy matter to remove some of the choke if the owner desires. Putting in choke, however, is more tricky and can only be done by a high-class gunsmith, who makes what is called 'recess choke'. Single-barrelled guns can be fitted with extension tubes which give variable degrees of choke. Some of them work fairly well but they all have the disadvantage of adding extra weight at the muzzle, just where it is *not* required if a gun is to handle well.

Singlepoint sight

This recently marketed device looks not unlike a telescopic sight as fitted on rifles. Indeed, its main purpose is for use on a rifle fired at a moving target, and this means in a warlike role. On looking through the sight, one sees a small luminous red spot apparently hanging in space. The rifleman keeps both eyes open, and the target seen by the left eye and the red spot seen by the right eye merge together. Provided that the optical axis of the sight is adjusted to the trajectory of the rifle, the user has only to put the spot on the target and fire in order to score a hit.

The sight can be used with a shotgun, although fitting it and zeroing it require considerable care. The gun's rib will have to be drilled and tapped to take a base block for the sight. Claims have been made that the sight makes shotgun shooting much easier – and, naturally, these claims have met with criticism on the grounds that such an instrument is unsporting and that, if used on a shotgun, it should be restricted to vermin shooting. Some good shots who have tried

[45]

the sight have found that it was accurate but 'picking up' the bird by eye was slower, although this may have been due in part to insufficient experience. The shooter must keep both eyes open. Claims that no forward allowance is necessary were not substantiated; the same lead as usual was required. Prospective buyers might be convinced of its value by a practical demonstration. The price is about £30.

Shotguns ought to be made to fit their users, but if you buy a ready-made gun it can be altered to fit you. The cost should be added to the initial price of the gun : about £25 for a session at a shooting school, including fitting, practice, instruction and cartridges and clays; and about £10–£30 for alterations to the stock, according to the time needed. The school will have a 'try-gun' which can be altered in bend, cast-off and length of stock, and the instructor can set these to your requirements and watch you shoot with it, making any minor alterations necessary. He will then take the measurements from the try-gun, and these are sent to the gunmaker to be applied to your own gun.

One normally uses a shotgun with both eyes open because with binocular vision it is easier to see the target and judge its range and course. In most cases, the right eye is 'master' – which means that its influence is stronger than the left eye; but if the left is master, complications ensue. You can test this by raising your right arm and pointing with your index finger at some object, both eyes being open. Now close your left eye. If your finger is still pointing at the object, your right eye is master. But if your finger points to the left of the object, it indicates that you have a left master-eye. This point must be established before any progress can be made with gun fitting.

[46]

To check, roughly, the fit of a gun, mount it fairly quickly at some mark, keeping both eyes open; or better still, use as a mark the tip of a friend's finger which he holds just in front of his eye. By closing your left eye, you can check where the gun is pointing – or if you have the help of a friend, he can tell you. If the gun points high, there is probably not enough bend in the stock; if low, there is too much bend. If the gun points left, you need more cast-off; and if to the right, the amount of cast-off should be reduced. See Plates 1 and 2 for what is meant by 'bend' and 'cast-off'. A stock which is too long will tend to catch in your clothing and you may have difficulty in reaching the triggers. With your arms in a normal position, a short stock will not bed into your shoulder; and when you fire, the recoil will cause some discomfort. If you point the gun at your own eye in a mirror, you can check its alignment along the barrels: the eye should be wholly visible and exactly along the rib. If you then refocus on to the rib, you should be able to see the whole of it.

Bend, and the height of the comb, affects the place above or below a target where the gun delivers its shot charge, when correctly held with the shooter's cheek pressed snugly on to the stock. When shooting at an aiming mark at forty yards range, two-thirds of the pattern should be above the mark. This helps to cure the tendency of most people to shoot below their birds. The amount of bend is partly determined by the length of the shooter's neck and the shape of his shoulders. Too much bend can be removed by slightly straightening the stock, provided that the gunmaker is satisfied that the wood will stand up to the treatment. Or the comb can be raised by sticking on to it a rubber strip, obtainable in varying thicknesses from gunsmiths. A better-looking job can be made in wood, after some experimenting with

[47]

the rubber comb-raisers. In some cases, the original bend may be satisfactory at the heel for fitting into the user's shoulder and should therefore not be altered. The cure, then, for shooting low is to build up the comb, which raises the backsight of the gun, the master-eye, and so brings up the muzzles. (Plate 21.)

If a gun has a fairly straight stock – that is, not much bend – it may shoot well for most shots but have a tendency to shoot high for low going-away shots, like a partridge or a hare. The cure would then be to leave the bend as it is but to reduce the toe of the butt, thus altering 'stand'. This is measured by holding the gun vertically with the toe and heel of the butt both on the ground and the breech touching a vertical post: the distance the muzzles are away from the post is the stand. On higher shots, the alteration in the toe would not have any effect because the shoulder is not then pressing hard against it.

All these points will be examined when you take your gun for fitting at the shooting school. Another detail the instructor will check is cast-off. This is a displacement of the butt to the right, away from the prolongation of an imaginary line back from the barrels. It compensates for the fact that the shoulder is farther to the right than is the master-eye. Shooting from the left shoulder requires cast-on; and shooting from the right shoulder but with a left master-eye calls for an across-eyed stock. It is possible that a man may have no master-eye, both eyes being equally assertive, in which case he will need considerable cast-off and what is known as a central-vision stock. (Plate 2.)

When the left eye tends to take control, perhaps particularly on shots taken to the left, the best solution is to close it partially as the shot is taken. But some people claim they cannot wink at all and do not seem inclined to learn. Of the alternatives available, wearing a black patch over the offending eye is not good because it allows only monocular vision and judging the range becomes difficult. If the shooter wears spectacles, he can place a small piece of sticking plaster about $\frac{1}{4}$-inch square on the left lens in such a position that the left eye cannot see along the barrels. Or a hand-guard can be fitted on the barrels, with a black disc sticking out to the left to interrupt sighting by the left eye. Some people even advocate raising the left thumb instead of laying it alongside the barrels, but this is not a very reliable method. An ingenious gadget is shown in Plate 19. The frame can be specially made by an optician, or adapted from Alpine sunglasses with a full-width tinted lens which can cover both eyes or be swivelled forward into a horizontal position, giving clear vision; the hinge on which it swings is sufficiently stiff to hold it firmly in any intermediate position. The modification consists in replacing the full-width lens with a smaller opaque piece of talc which will cover only the left eye. In use, the eye is not covered but the talc is swung forward a little below horizontal. The wearer then has full use of both eyes for walking about, loading his gun etc. and even watching an approaching bird; but as soon as he mounts his gun, the opaque talc blocks the view along the barrels to his left eye. (Plate 20.) This device has been given considerable testing in the field and it is most efficient.

Young people see out of the centre of the eye's pupil, but as they grow older they often have a tendency to look out of the inner corner of the eye. This slight displacement of the line of sight causes the shooter to move the gun barrels over to the left, and he thus misses his target. A shooting school coach can spot this fault and correct it by slightly increasing the cast-off of the gun. The moral here is that gun fitting is not for life: as a man gets older, and probably fatter – and certainly as his eyesight changes in middle age – a few slight alterations in the fit of his gun are needed, and their effect can be surprisingly helpful.

When a gun is taken to a gunsmith for some obvious repair, other faults are often found which the owner has either ignored or knows nothing about. Some guns which come in for repair are in a most frighteningly dangerous state. One desperate habit, which is by no means uncommon, is for the owner of a gun whose top lever spring has broken to 'fix' it in position with a rubber band. This can allow the gun to open on firing and the charge to blow back into the shooter's face. Ribs are often found loose – not dangerously so, but sufficient for water to get in below them and cause rusting, which may eventually eat into the barrel and could result in a burst. Trigger pulls are frequently far too light in an old gun; wear, particularly in the bent, can result in a pull of only about 2 lbs. being sufficient to fire the gun, which may also go off when it is jarred without a trigger being pulled at all. Sometimes the action of closing the gun is sufficient to release the tumbler and fire the gun. These faults may develop earlier in cheap foreign guns, which incorporate case-hardened mild steel instead of cast steel as used in English guns; when the hardening wears off, the gun will require an overhaul and this will be a good deal sooner than with a better made gun. The lumps on the barrels, which fit into the action, may be loose, in which case the gun will have to be re-proved; 'loose' is a comparative term and a gunsmith uses it in conditions where the ignorant gun owner would probably not notice it at all. Similarly, the fore-end loop – that projection below the barrels which secures it – can be loose and cause trouble with the ejectors. The stock can be cracked, often along a line of the chequering on the hand unseen by the owner.

[50]

Dents in the barrels should be obvious to the owner but are frequently ignored, and he probably does not know about the bulge which forms round a dent. They ought to be removed at once, before they grow worse. If the action is loose, as described earlier in this chapter when considering buying a second-hand gun, it becomes progressively worse every time the gun is fired; neglecting to have it repaired is like never changing the oil in a car.

These are the sort of faults which may be discovered by a gunsmith when the gun is given to him, perhaps just for some obvious job like reblueing the barrels. An awareness of what can go wrong should emphasise the need for having the gun overhauled regularly: every year if it is used hard throughout the season, and every two or three years otherwise. Some gun accidents could undoubtedly be prevented if guns had to be checked and certified as safe in the same way that cars over three years old have to be.

The standard cartridge for our standard gun may be taken as having a $2\frac{1}{2}$-inch crimped case loaded with $1\frac{1}{16}$ oz. of No. 6 shot. But cartridge length, load and shot size can vary according to many requirements. A 2-inch cartridge with a $\frac{7}{8}$ oz. load has less recoil and might be chosen for a lady, or perhaps for someone who is prone to gun headache after firing a large number of rounds. Longer cartridges of $2\frac{3}{4}$-inch or 3-inch contain a bigger shot load and are used for serious clay pigeon competitions and for wildfowling.

Most modern cartridges of British manufacture are described by the gauge size and by the length of gun chamber in which they are intended to be used, the description appearing on the cartridge box and sometimes also on the individual cartridge. The description does not refer to the actual length of the cartridge. This sounds confusing but

[51]

it arises from the introduction a few years ago of crimped closed cartridges instead of rolled turnover; a crimp closure caused the loaded cartridge to be shorter than before, and it was possible to fit a heavy-load cartridge into the chambers of a gun only proved for a lighter load. The gun would thus be subjected to higher pressures, which could be dangerous.

The length of a cartridge is not the same as the length of the chamber; but with rolled turnover cartridges, the length of the *fired case* is the same as the length of the chamber. With some crimp closure cartridges the length of the fired case is actually longer than the gun chamber. For instance, a number of 12-bore cartridges intended for $2\frac{1}{2}$-inch chambers have cases which are $2\frac{3}{4}$ inches long. There are two reasons for this: with a case of $2\frac{9}{16}$ inches long (12-bore $2\frac{1}{2}$-inch chambers are actually $2\frac{9}{16}$ long), the finished cartridge is only $2\frac{1}{16}$ inches long when crimp closed, as some of the tube is used for the closure. With such a short cartridge, it is not always possible to accommodate the necessary length of wadding column for satisfactory ballistics, and so a longer case is necessary. The other reason concerns the correct functioning in auto-loading weapons. Many of these will feed only those loaded cartridges which are the same length as the old rolled turnover cartridges; a $2\frac{3}{4}$-inch case with a crimped closure gives this same length loaded as a $2\frac{9}{16}$-inch case with rolled turnover. There is no danger in using such cartridges with $2\frac{3}{4}$-inch cases in a $2\frac{1}{2}$-inch chambered weapon because the loading of the cartridge is adjusted so that the ballistic level is satisfactory.

$2\frac{1}{2}$-inch cartridges are obviously made for $2\frac{1}{2}$-inch chambered guns, but they can safely be used in $2\frac{3}{4}$-inch guns. They often are when the owner of a $2\frac{3}{4}$-inch gun bought it because he wants the bigger shot load for wildfowling but likes to use cheaper $2\frac{1}{2}$-inch cartridges when he is, for instance, pigeon shooting. But cartridges *intended* for $2\frac{3}{4}$-inch chambers have higher pressure and they should not be used in $2\frac{1}{2}$-inch guns. Similarly, cartridges intended for 3-inch chambers must not be used in shorter ones.

Progressive-burning powders permit heavier shot loads than were common twenty years ago, and some American cartridges are loaded with $1\frac{5}{8}$ oz. in $2\frac{3}{4}$-inch cases and $1\frac{7}{8}$ oz. in 3-inch cases. These can generate alarmingly high pressures in guns not designed for them. In 1967, Imperial Metal Industries (Kynoch) Ltd., best known of British cartridge manufacturers, under the brand name of 'Eley', brought to the market their magnum cartridges. These have $1\frac{1}{2}$ oz. of shot in the $2\frac{3}{4}$-inch size and $1\frac{5}{8}$ oz. in the 3-inch size, and they created a certain stir, especially among the more sensible owners of 'Magnums' – which in this case means not an extra large bottle of champagne but a 3-inch chambered gun used for wildfowling. The new cartridges generated pressures higher than those for which most guns of similar chamber lengths were nitro-proved. The magnum cartridges can cause pressures up to $3\frac{1}{2}$ and 4 tons per square inch respectively. Since 1955, the maximum service pressure for which a gun has been proved has been marked on the flats of the barrels (underneath, at the breech end), but earlier guns are not so marked. If, therefore, you own a gun proved before 1955 you should check the service pressure which it can take before using magnum cartridges. In fact, your old Magnum 3-inch gun, if in proof, will be safe with the $2\frac{3}{4}$-inch magnum cartridges, but it will require reproof before using the 3-inch ones. When a gun is sent for a test proof, the barrels must first be prepared by a gunsmith, who will ensure that they are really straight and will remove any dents; the gun will also be stripped and cleaned and the total cost is likely to be about £60. The owner of an oldish Magnum may well consider this price, and the possibility of his gun failing proof, not worth while and so be content with restricting himself to $2\frac{3}{4}$-inch magnum cartridges.

The main current Eley 12-bore game cartridges are listed below:

Use	Name	Shot charge oz.	Suitable for guns with chamber length of	and proved for pressures of
Ultra light load	Two inch	$\frac{7}{8}$	2 inch	$2\frac{1}{4}$ tons
Light load	Impax	1	$2\frac{1}{2}$ inch	3 tons
Normal game load	Grand Prix	$1\frac{1}{16}$	$2\frac{1}{2}$ inch	3 tons
Slightly bigger game load	Grand Prix HV	$1\frac{1}{8}$	$2\frac{1}{2}$ inch	3 tons
Biggest load in $2\frac{1}{2}$-inch case, for wildfowling or high pheasants	Maximum	$1\frac{3}{16}$	$2\frac{1}{2}$ inch	3 tons
Bigger load, without gun being too heavy	Hymax	$1\frac{1}{4}$	$2\frac{3}{4}$ inch	$3\frac{1}{4}$ tons
As Hymax but slightly more expensive	Alphamax	$1\frac{1}{4}$	$2\frac{3}{4}$ inch	$3\frac{1}{4}$ tons
Magnum, but $2\frac{3}{4}$ inch case	Magnum 70	$1\frac{1}{2}$	$2\frac{3}{4}$ inch	$3\frac{1}{2}$ tons
Heavier wildfowling gun, 3-inch case	Magnum 75	$1\frac{5}{8}$	3 inch	4 tons

The important point is that most British cartridges are described by the length of gun chamber for which they are intended. The actual length of a cartridge case, empty or loaded, cannot be taken as a guide. Eley cartridges have a warning on the box about gun chamber lengths as well as the service pressures on which the Proof House pressures are based for testing weapons. If you use strange cartridges, particularly foreign-made ones, you should ensure that your gun is proved for whatever pressures they generate.

Increasing the load in a cartridge does not increase its range anything like as much as some people think. It has been calculated that an extra $\frac{1}{4}$ oz. of shot, with appropriate powder, increases the effective range by only about 4 yards – and this, of course, is too small an amount to be measured by eye. If you buy some $1\frac{1}{2}$ oz. cartridges, you should not imagine that you can shoot them at duck 10 or 15 yards farther away than you could with a $1\frac{1}{4}$ oz. load. Extra loads do give some gain in range, comparing $1\frac{1}{16}$ oz. with $1\frac{5}{8}$ oz., for instance; but their main object is to provide more pellets and better patterns, particularly when larger shot is demanded for wildfowling. At maximum range, therefore, they do give a better chance of a kill; but we should all beware of thinking that their range is *much* greater and of taking shots at birds which are so far away that they will only be wounded.

The term 'high velocity' may lead beginners to think that cartridges of this description reach their target so much quicker that they will hit it even if the man behind the gun is a bit slow in his swing and fails to give enough forward allowance. Such is not the case. The mean velocity of a standard cartridge over 20 yards is about 1070 feet per second and of a high velocity cartridge about 1130 feet per second. This small difference will not miraculously turn misses into hits.

It is important to know how much powder and how much

shot such cartridges contain: if they have more powder and less shot, they will produce a worse pattern than a standard cartridge. They can be a help, accepting the stronger recoil, in well-choked guns used for Olympic Trench or wildfowling. But any shooter changing to these cartridges should check that his gun gives as good a pattern with them as with those he normally uses. With a lightly choked gun, the pattern may well be worse.

Patterns are normally checked at 40 yards, firing at a whitewashed steel plate and counting the number of pellet marks in a 30-inch circle. There are theoretical figures of the number of pellets which should appear with various loads and with different degrees of choke. Incidentally, any such test of a gun or cartridges must be done carefully and methodically: not by just banging off a couple of shots at a piece of newspaper pinned to a barn door. A perfect pattern is something which has so far eluded the makers of guns and cartridges. It should have all the pellets evenly distributed and the majority of them within the 30-inch circle, taking into account range, load and degree of choke. But no such pattern exists, because there are always gaps. If we take a gap of 5 inches diameter as being unacceptable, because most game birds could escape through it without being hit in a vulnerable place, tests show that there can often be a remarkable number of such gaps. At 40 yards, the right barrel of an improved-cylinder 12-bore firing $1\frac{1}{16}$ oz. of shot should give 144 pellets in the 30-inch circle, and the pattern will quite likely show as many as six 5-inch-diameter gaps. This imperfection may come as a surprise; but it does emphasise that the number of pellets in a pattern is of less importance than its evenness, which may often be of poor quality. The number of pellets *is* important, of course; but remember that pattern fails

[56]

before penetration. Tables are available to show the striking energy in foot-pounds of individual pellets at various ranges – but it is no help if one pellet has sufficient energy at 45 yards to kill a pheasant, hitting it in the right place, if the gun which fires it cannot produce a good enough pattern beyond 35 yards with sufficient pellets to ensure a kill.

A more tightly choked barrel will give a denser pattern, but concentrated nearer the middle part of the 30-inch circle, and there will be several gaps near the circumference of the circle. The effect of a considerable degree of choke is to give more range in the sense of holding the majority of the pellets closer together for a longer period; but an unwanted result of the constriction of the shot as it leaves the muzzle is that more of the pellets become deformed and spoil the outside edges of the pattern. At 30 yards the pattern from a true cylinder is as dense as that from a half choke at 40 yards and it is a better quality pattern, with a more even spread of shot across the whole of the 30-inch circle. It is a better game-killing pattern, especially as 30 yards is, in practice quite a long range. A great deal of game is shot at ranges of about 20 to 25 yards. The lesson here is that we should not use guns more tightly choked than we need for the majority of our shooting. When you meet the owner of an old gun – often a farmer or a gamekeeper – he sometimes speaks of it as a 'hard hitting gun'. The reason for his undoubtedly effective shooting with it is very likely that it is fairly open bored: the original choke is partly worn away and the gun throws very good patterns at the range at which he takes most of his shots, about 20 yards.

All guns should be regulated before they are sold, but only the better ones are. The process starts by firing several shots at the pattern plate and comparing the pellet count with the theoretical figure. Often, a gun does not shoot as it measures. A barrel may rate improved cylinder when measured but shoot patterns with a pellet-count equivalent to full choke. The gunsmith must then alter the choke and try again until he has regulated the gun to fire the sort of pattern required by its owner. Very few guns shoot as they measure, and some surprising anomalies occur. In one extreme case, a gun by a famous maker shot choke patterns from the right barrel and improved cylinder ones from the left – although the measurements showed the borings the other way round, as one would expect. No amount of regulating could cure this gun and eventually new barrels were made for it. Regulating a gun may cost from £25 to £35, but if the work is necessary it will be worthwhile. (Plates 26, 27.)

Some owners, however, having acquired the proverbial 'little knowledge', may be inclined to demand unnecessary alterations to their guns. If a gun is suspected of not giving good patterns, it can be tested and regulated. After that, it is up to the user to point it straight. For example, an owner whose gun was bored improved cylinder in the right barrel thought that it gave far too open a pattern, causing him to miss. He decided to buy another gun more tightly choked, but first he took his current gun to a shooting school. The pattern on the plate looked all right, but the owner said to the instructor: 'Theory doesn't always work out in practice, and this gun is a poor killer. I bet you can't hit fifteen out of twenty-five clays with it. Bet you a fiver!'

'All right. But we'll make it twenty clays. I'll take them from the trap for the going-away shot, where the clay is a pretty small target with its edge towards you. But I won't take your money.'

They went over to the trap and the instructor killed twenty-five clays in a row. There was nothing wrong with the gun as long as its pattern was kept on the target.

Those who use smaller bored guns, such as 16- or 20-bore, are not always aware of the fact that they throw approximately the same diameter of shot pattern as a 12-bore. The difference in patterns is not their size but the number of pellets in them, and this is naturally less with the smaller bores. It may be salutory to realise that the diameter of the spread of the main part of the shot charge of a shotgun, irrespective of its bore, is only 26 inches at 20 yards with improved cylinder, 21 inches with half choke, and only 16 inches with full choke. This has nothing to do with the 30-inch circle, which is an arbitrary size used for assessing patterns at various ranges. So if you are going to shoot at comparatively close but still average ranges of 20 yards with a well-choked barrel, you have to point it accurately to score a hit at all. And when you do, the game will probably be badly smashed. Large shot, 4's or 5's, big heavy magnum guns and full choke may at first seem more likely to be successful; they also have an appeal like fast motor bikes and sports cars. There is no harm in it and it can be lots of fun. But for most ordinary game shooting, it is hard to beat the effectiveness of our standard $6\frac{1}{2}$ lb. gun, bored true cylinder and half choke and firing $1\frac{1}{16}$ oz. of No. 6 shot. If any brawny youngster thinks this sounds sissy, he might like to try an American Winchester single-barrelled gun which made its debut in 1968. Called the 370, it is available in various bores and barrel lengths from 30 to 36 inches. The advertising blurb encourages he-men like this:

'Concern has been expressed that this new gun, which weighs but six pounds, may kick when fired with the 3-inch, $1\frac{7}{8}$ oz. magnum load.

[59]

You're mighty well told it will kick !
On a straight overhead shot, the gun should drive a man
into the gumbo mud to the tops of his five-buckle boots.
This is an honest-injun, salty-dog type gun that will bug
your eyes, drain your sinuses, and restore your regularity.
From either end it packs authority.
Every boy should shoot this gun at least once.'

Whatever sort of gun you have, it is the cartridge that
produces the shot which kills the bird. It is nearly always a
false economy to buy cheap cartridges for serious shooting.
Only good cartridges made under carefully controlled
factory conditions can maintain a really consistent standard.
The best way to get cheaper cartridges is to buy them in
bulk as gun clubs and shooting syndicates sometimes do, dis-
tributing them to members at a discount price. A box of
twenty-five game cartridges cost, in 1981, £3, but bought
5000 at a time the cost comes down by five per cent. Home-
loading saves money, of course, but a good loading press
costs a minimum of £50. A practised operator can make
himself about 100 cartridges an hour. Provided that he can
buy his powder and shot in bulk and obtain free cases by
collecting other people's discarded ones, his cost for a box of
twenty-five could be from about £2.

The question of the dangers with home-loaded cartridges
depends on the care, and perhaps intelligence, of the maker.
Not everyone contemplating home-loading is aware of the
several components of a cartridge and of the exactitude required in measuring powder and shot. Nor of the fact that
if the weight of powder is increased by five per cent the
induced pressure will possibly be increased by from ten to
fifteen per cent. If the wad is changed, for one reason or
another, the powder ought to be reduced by ten per cent for

initial safety. And there is the vital matter of distinguishing between grains and avoirdupois drams and apothecaries' drachms. If you do start making your own cartridges, it is worth the small fee to send a few samples to be checked by the Proof House authorities, who will give you details of loading weights, muzzle velocity, pressures and recoil, etc. Some useful notes on the reloading of cartridges can be obtained from Imperial Metal Industries (Kynoch) Ltd., Eley Ammunition Division, Witton, Birmingham, 6.

Home-loaded cartridges will do for fairly unimportant occasions such as pigeon shooting, but they cannot reach the standard of consistency of good factory-made ones. For an important occasion – perhaps an invitation to shoot pheasants, or even a wildfowling trip, when the opportunity of a shot is likely to be sufficiently rare for one to want to make sure that, whatever excuse there may be for missing, at least the cartridge is not to blame – even a good home-loader would probably feel more confident with some factory-made cartridges.

Plastic, or polyethylene, is now used for cartridge cases, although the normal paper case is still made and preferred by some shooting men. Plastic cases are the best choice for home-loaders, but their non-destructibility makes them an added untidiness to the countryside. Like fishermen's plastic sandwich and bait-bags on the river bank, they lie around for ever – unless some altruistic chap picks them up. The danger to livestock from empty plastic cases is minimal. Tests have shown that cases placed among food in a pig-trough have been untouched by the animals when they had finished all the food. Cartridge cases have been found, however, which have been nibbled by some small creatures, possibly rats or squirrels. Whether they ate any pieces and died is not known.

[61]

Plastic cases are waterproof, stronger than paper ones and easier to store in bulk at cartridge factories. They will probably supersede paper ones before very long. There have been, however, a number of complaints about them – not all justified. One which does seem true is that after a large number of plastic cartridges have been fired a deposit sometimes accumulates in the walls of the gun's chambers, especially if the chambers have not been properly cleaned. This may be due to tiny particles of dirt being attracted to the cartridge case by static electricity and subsequently deposited on the chamber walls under the pressure of firing. It does not occur with paper cases.

Incidentally, not everyone realises how far shotgun pellets can travel. The extreme range occurs when the gun is pointed up at an angle of from 30° to 33° – not 45°, as is commonly supposed; 45° would give maximum range only in a vacuum. Generally speaking, extreme range is about 250 yards, and when fired vertically No. 6 shot goes up about 120 yards. Shot pattering down has hardly any damaging effect. All the same, it is as well to know just how far away your shotgun and cartridges might at least cause some alarm among people going innocently about their business.

CHAPTER THREE

COMPETITION

'YOUR bird, sir', he said with a smile, doffing his cap to the Gun on his right. The other looked up briefly from reloading, and then got ready for his next shot. They had both fired at that last bird and our polite friend was more than a little certain that he was fractionally first, and that the bird crumpled immediately. But it was a 'shared' bird and his reaction was to award it to the other Gun, be he never so taciturn. . . .

Good manners never come amiss, and in the shooting field they contribute to the enjoyment of the day in a subtle but vital way, even if only in reminiscence. It makes no difference whether the occasion is the most formal of 'Big Day' pheasant shoots or just a couple of friends walking-up a bit of rough ground with a spaniel. Politeness, and a desire to help others to have a good day too, is essential if the full value is to be gained from any day in the country, whatever the sport. This is always so, but it is most happily found among shooting people. The making of a good day never depends on the numbers in the bag, although no one, least of all the keeper and the host, would deny the importance of this aspect. The day depends on good company and good fun in the best sense of the word, whether it is barracking old Charlie, the beater, who fell off the plank bridge over Dingle Brook, or ribbing Sir Charles who missed that jay with both barrels at the end of the drive, in front of all the beaters and most of the Guns. It is more than likely that both of them will laugh over each incident at the end of the day.

A competitive spirit should never arise in the game shooting field. On those sad occasions when it does, the culprit rarely does himself any good. All the same, when a bird goes to one Gun but is also near enough to another to be shootable, the second Gun should watch it carefully *over the muzzles* and be ready to shoot if number one either fails to fire or does so and misses. If number two just watches the bird with his gun idly over his arm, by the time he sees that he can have a go he will be too late to make a correct preparation for the shot. It is more than likely that he will just throw up his gun and miss. If he does get his gun to his shoulder and then has a doubt whether the bird is his or not, it is practically certain that his swing will be checked and the bird missed. Therefore, if a bird comes your way and you decide it *is* yours, go the whole hog and shoot it. If you have made a mistake and it should have been left to your neighbour, then immediately apologise. If in doubt, follow the bird over your gun muzzles until you are sure. This emphasises the teaching in Chapter One, 'the eye over the muzzles', which stresses that whenever a shooter looks about him at probable targets his body should pivot in the required direction and his gun muzzles should follow his eye. (Plate 9.)

A fairly innocent form of competition, although one that breeds a silly self-deception, arises in talk of kills to cartridges. Even shooters who would like to be honest with themselves and their friends do not appreciate the large number of cartridges fired compared with the head of game in the bag. An interesting test was made by an onlooker at a pheasant stand who had one of those game counters which

[64]

THE CHEEK ON THE STOCK
21. The cheek is pressed tightly on to the stock. The comb has been raised by sticking on a rubber strip, to make the gun shoot higher.

GAMEKEEPER'S CLAY PIGEON SHOOT
22. A nice style; feet, weight, arms, head, all in the right position.

THE SECOND BARREL
23. He kills his first bird with the right barrel.

THE BUTT OFF THE SHOULDER
24. As he lines up the muzzles on a second bird he takes the butt off his shoulder, lowering it a few inches.

BUTT ON AGAIN FOR LEFT BARREL
25. He swings on round, "reading" a different bird, and then brings the butt up again for the second shot.

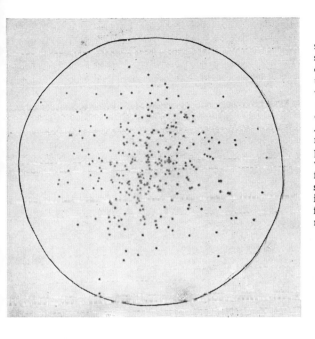

PELLET PATTERNS: A BIT TIGHT

26. The right barrel, supposedly improved cylinder, at 20 yards. A tight pattern which would tend to miss completely at this range or smash any bird it hit. At 40 yards the barrel might give quite a good pattern, but the owner wants one barrel for fairly close-range work, such as pigeon dropping in to decoys. He asked for his gun to be regulated

THE PATTERN OPENED UP

27. After regulating, the same barrel gave this pattern at 20 yards. It is an improvement and although the pattern might be rather open at 40 yards the left barrel, at half-choke, will take care of longer range shots

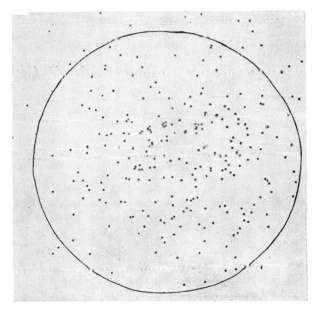

28. Grouse coveys tend to pack together later in the season. But the shooter

BRAILING

29. The keeper holds a cock pheasant brailed with a leather strap on its right wing.

THE INCUBATOR

30. The keeper checks his incubator as the chicks, in this case partridges, begin to hatch.

THE REARING FIELD

31. The keeper feeds young pheasants in July, whistling to them so that they become accustomed to the sound. The same whistle will call them to feed after they have been released in the coverts.

A TRAP FOR A MAGPIE

32. The keeper made this trap, with an artificial nest in it baited with a dummy egg. Magpies are egg stealers.

ROUGH SHOOTERS' DOGS

33. These dogs play a vital part in contributing to the bag.

A RIGHT AND LEFT

. remarkable picture of two pheasants falling, a right and left by a first-class shot, who
ing his second gun from his loader. A self-opener helps in the speed needed to reload.

Retrieving a Runner
36. A labrador brings in a winged
grouse. This bird, scuttling away
and hiding in the heather, would
have been almost impossible to
find without a dog.

registers a number each time the button is pressed: he used it to count the shots. He was clicking away every time he heard a bang and at the end of the drive the counter read 188. They were a good team of Guns, but the number of pheasants picked up was 41. On another occasion, the head keeper on a big shoot knew that the lunch-time bag was 460. He ordered the collection of all the cartridge cases lying around by the pegs on the three drives. When they were brought in and counted, there were about 1500 of them.

Loaders can tell you accurate figures as long as there is sufficient time after the drive for most of the pick-up to be completed before they and their Guns are whisked off by Land-Rovers. You might hear something like :

'My chap was number two. A lot of birds came our way and he fired a hundred and twenty-five cartridges. We picked up forty-three birds.'

or

'The birds show well at this stand. Many of them are pretty high. We'll watch the shooting for a while . . . Twenty-five shots fired, and not a bird hit so far ! I wonder what the Guns will say about that?'

or

A asks B how he fared as walking gun. 'Got a couple,' says B, 'and missed one.' Sounds quite good, doesn't it? Although, actually, B killed each of his birds with a second barrel and also fired both barrels at the one he missed: so his score was two out of six.

You can keep your own honest score by counting your cartridges at the beginning and end of the day and making a note of the number of birds you kill at each stand – unless things become very hectic and you lose count. If you then divide the total bag by the number of Guns, you will know whether you have contributed the right proportion com-

[65]

pared with the others. There was once a shrewd host who, at the end of the day, used to ask each of his Guns how many birds they had shot. When he added up their replies, the total was invariably more than the total bag – which shows that it is quite difficult to be honest in these matters.

Boasting about shooting skill is fortunately rare, but a little self-deception is almost always present. If you hear someone claiming to have shot remarkably straight, it is quite possible that he honestly believes his claim. But if you know how often good shots miss, you may feel a little less sad about your own performance. Newcomers to shooting frequently suppose that the old hands kill practically everything that comes near them, but this is not so. One kill to four cartridges is quite a good average performance over all types of shot and different conditions of shooting. Much higher averages are achieved at some pheasant drives, perhaps when the birds are not too difficult or when they are so plentiful that the Gun can pick the shots he likes and leave the ones he knows he is liable to miss. First-class shots, however, take everything as it comes; and some of them are fantastically accurate. There is the story of a wager made between an Indian rajah and an English earl on a famous Hampshire shoot just before the turn of the century. Each was to try to shoot a hundred pheasants at the main drive of the day, the winner being he who used fewest cartridges. The rajah killed his hundred with a hundred shots. The earl ran him very close: he missed his hundredth bird but killed it with the second barrel.

Such shooting is exceptional, and must have been even in those days when Sir Ralph Payne-Gallwey – a most experienced shot in all parts of the United Kingdom – was observing and noting all manner of details. He conducted experiments on guns and ballistics and the resistance to shot of high pheasants; he invented gadgets to help shooters; and he wrote several books, including *Shooting* in the Badminton Library. When he published his findings of the sort of averages which ought to be achieved by a good shot under all conditions his figures were: average, 30 kills for 100 cartridges; good, 35 for 100; very good, 40 for 100; and first-class, 45 for 100 cartridges.

Where competition is expected to flourish all the time is in clay pigeon shooting, which is a sport of its own and one about which many game shooters remain obstinately ignorant. As competitive shooting, it is most demanding – particularly in the high degree of concentration necessary. The participant must ignore his surroundings, the spectators, and the extraneous noise of aircraft or trains. He must compress his whole being into just one job: breaking the next clay.

When Bob Braithwaite returned to England after winning an Olympic Gold Medal in 1968, several of the interviewing reporters, like their readers, knew very little about this sport which had suddenly become news. One of them asked:

'I believe you shoot the clays in twenty-fives, isn't that right?'

The reply was: 'No, in ones. There is only *one* bird all day – the next.'

Interest in clay pigeon shooting is growing and the standard is improving. '100 straight' – which means one hundred kills without a miss – used to be comparatively rare, but now there may be several such scores at a Down-The-Line meeting. In Down-The-Line the gun is held to the shoulder and the shooter calls to the trapper that he is ready for the clay bird to be released.

Olympic Trench is a more difficult form of competition, one offering a greater challenge. It is such a specialised

[67]

business that the ordinary game shot would be quite lost if he tried it without previous practice at easier targets. Even the experts rarely manage a 100-straight. The sporting lay-out, with its driven partridges and high pheasants and running rabbits, offers good practice for game shooting and, to a lesser degree, so does Skeet. In both these events the gun must be held down while the shooter waits for the clay to appear, with the butt below the elbow and not up at the shoulder in the somewhat unnatural way permitted in Down-the-Line and Olympic Trench. Incidentally, as an example of the high standard now reached in most countries where clay shooting is taken seriously, at the American Skeet Championships in 1968 twenty-five competitors had a 'possible' of 250 kills out of 250 birds. In the shoot-off to decide the winner, two competitors were still in after break-ing a further 800 clays without a miss. Then they decided to call it a draw.

Some non-participants believe that clay pigeon shooting is of no help to game shooting, but this is a rather bigoted outlook. It is the only way to practise shooting. The criticism that the clays slow down and stop is scarcely relevant since they should always be taken early in their flight, when they are moving fast. The counterclaim to this argument is that pheasants slow down, too, and stop to feed or go to roost – but we do not wait that long to shoot them. In fact, a clay slowing down towards the end of its flight is nearly always *not* an easy shot. Those who think it is usually miss when they try to prove their point.

Serious competitive clay pigeon shooting is a specialist subject, calling for both technique and equipment of a different form from that required for normal game shooting. An ordinary game gun, however, is satisfactory for the simple, not very serious shoots arranged by small gun clubs.

[68]

These are always good fun, and the competitors learn to concentrate and shoot in company without feeling shy or nervous. Such shoots also provide opportunities for studying varieties of style – provided, of course, that the student remembers to watch the performer on the ground and not just stare at the clays in the sky. The mild competition of club shoots encourages a man to try to do better, to find out where he fails and so improve his skill. In the shooting field, it is too easy to criticise, mentally, when watching another man shoot. But if you go to a club shoot on a sporting layout you can think such thoughts and then go and put yourself in the other fellow's shoes – often a most salutory experience.

To watch a National Championship for the first time is quite an eye-opener when one observes the extreme and almost ruthless efficiency of the best shots. No shooting man should consider himself fully experienced until he has attended a top-class meeting, for there is always an instructional interest in watching any sport superbly well performed even if one has no ambition to do as well oneself. Some of the more dedicated clay shooters have no interest in game shooting, but most of them enjoy it and are very good shots. But they will tell you that live-bird shooting is, without any doubt at all, much more difficult.

Readers of *Clay Pigeon Marksmanship* will know that this is a developing sport with changes being made from time to time. In 1967, the Clay Pigeon Shooting Association changed the scoring system for Down-The-Line from "2 and 1" to "3 and 2", giving three points for a first-barrel kill and two points for a second-barrel kill. Universal Trench is now shot as an economical way of practising for Olympic Trench. The layout consists of five traps placed in a trench. The traps can be set to throw clays on certain defined trajectories; but once having been set, they remain fixed during a shoot.

[69]

After the 1968 Olympic Games, draft rules were adopted by the International Shooting Union for a new form of competition provisionally called Automatic Trap. A special trap is used which constantly weaves up and down, as well as from side to side, and fires off the clays in whatever direction it happens to be pointing when the shot is called. The device is in use in some clubs and is generally known as Ball Trap.

Dogs are discussed in Chapter Five, but into this section come field trials and working tests. Many shooting men have never witnessed either of these, and other luckier ones have only done so as Guns. Field trials come in for a good deal of criticism – particularly of the kind that the dogs require too much help from their handlers, that they are almost 'circus animals' and are not much good on a real shooting day. Not everyone can afford the time to look after a dog, and those who live in cities can hardly keep a gundog even if they want to; but it is unfair for non-dog-owners, who would be quite incapable of handling field trial dogs, to suggest that they are of little practical use in the shooting field. Some of the criticism levelled at field trials arises from the fact that nearly all the shooting is done walking-up, whereas most practical retriever work consists of picking up after drives. There is bound to be some artificiality at field trials if dogs are to be tested fairly in similar conditions of ground and cover, but they are the best method of testing and proving the essential qualities required of a gundog. The indications are that more attention may soon be paid to testing dogs for steadiness during a drive, for whining, and for the courage to face denser cover than usually met when walking-up.

Another discussion point arises from the cry: 'Field trials

[70]

aren't natural because the handlers can concentrate entirely on their dogs. If they had to shoot as well, it would be much better.' It is quite true that controlling a dog is far easier if you are not carrying a gun, because even the best-trained animal can sense when his handler's attention is distracted and he may be tempted to take advantage of it.

Although field trials would be more convincing if the handlers were to shoot over their own dogs, there are two major snags to this. Firstly, if it is a private shoot, the owner of the ground where the trials are held will naturally want to field his own team of Guns; and if it is a syndicate, the members will probably insist on enjoying the shooting themselves. Field trials are entirely dependent on the generosity of the owners of shooting rights.

The second disadvantage is that the results might be unfair to the dogs. The good shot could 'play crafty' and shoot the birds when he wished, probably killing most of them stone dead and dropping them where he thought was most suitable for his dog. The dud shot would miss many birds, which would not help to keep his dog steady, and he would probably have several difficult runners. An unbiased team of neutral Guns who are out simply to enjoy their shooting provides the only way to ensure that, as far as possible, all the dogs have a fair chance. There is already quite an element of luck in these trials, and the organisers and judges are always trying to avoid anything which might tend to favour certain competitors.

The preliminary to field trials is the working test, usually carried out in the summer, when dummies are used instead of live game. Such a test is very helpful to the young dog and its aspiring handler, who is probably its owner as well. Many field trial dogs are handled by professionals, which is not as odd as may first appear. After all, the owner of a racehorse usually employs someone else to ride it for him. The warning which owners of successful dogs in working tests should heed is that there is a very big step up when the dog enters the field trial world. Formerly, the dog worked on ground devoid of the distracting scent of live game. But in the field trial, it is asked to respond to its handler's commands in conditions reeking of the most exciting scent it can experience. The result can be a perplexingly wild and uncontrollable dog and a terrible disappointment for its handler. The safeguard is to work the dog frequently on game shooting days before attempting field trials, and an excellent way to do this is to go picking-up – of which more is said in Chapter Seven. If you want to attend a field trial, you will find future lists in the weekly papers *The Field* and *Shooting Times*.

Competitive dog work undoubtedly makes for better dogs and improves the breed. There is very little money in it directly and, like clay pigeon shooting, the prizes scarcely pay for the expenses. All shooting men owe much of the pleasure they enjoy to gundogs, even if the dogs which retrieve their birds belong to someone else. And many of the best gundogs have in their breeding an ancestor whose capabilities were developed by running in field trials.

While being wholly deplorable during actual game shooting with other people – except, perhaps, for a light-hearted wager – competition makes for improvement. Just as racing instead of merely cruising improves the skill of a yachtsman, so the urge to do better than others can help the shooter. But he must remember his manners and modesty.

A certain man was a member of a syndicate and was known to be critical of all but himself. After a day's shooting when the Guns were having tea at the lodge while the

keeper and the shoot manager counted the bag and distributed some of it among the cars, this fellow was boasting
about his prowess and how well he had shot, despite what
he reckoned was poor organisation of the day by the manager. 'He has no idea, that chap,' he said. 'He made such a
nonsense of it all that I could have shot him!'

One of the others present murmured, 'I don't believe you
could.'

CHAPTER FOUR

THE GAMEKEEPER

THE good gamekeeper with long service on a shoot knows practically everything there is to know about it. He also has a keen awareness of what goes on among his Guns on a shooting day – and his knowledge of them is nearly always greater than theirs of him. His opinions of them are, of course, kept strictly under his hat, although just occasionally a hint may be exposed, discernible to any but the thick-skinned.

One of these unfortunates was a regular guest on a shoot in the West Country, where he had something of a reputation as a know-all and a selfish but not very efficient shot. On an informal day after Christmas, when some of the tenant farmers were out, and one or two schoolboys on holiday, the keeper was also carrying a gun. The self-styled Big Shot suggested that the keeper should take his place with the Guns on one drive, rather than control the beaters, and try 'some driven game, instead of just plugging the easy ones as they break back'. So the keeper did; and he could see that BS, who was next to him, was not shooting at all well. In fact, he was obviously better at shooting a line than shooting game. Earlier on, BS had spoken of woodcock and opined that they were certainly difficult birds. *He* wouldn't waste cartridges on them while they were dodging about in the trees. 'In the open, of course, they're quite easy. But difficult to find, you know, even the best dogs usually won't pick 'em up.'

Right at the end of the drive, a woodcock got up at the

edge of the covert and flew between the keeper and BS. 'Yours!' shouted BS, and then fired at it himself with both barrels – and missed. The bird swerved towards the keeper, who shot it, held out his hand and caught it as it fell.

Perhaps some of the beaters may have been grinning a little as the keeper walked across to BS and said, 'Yours, sir?'

Keepers are often reputed to be good shots, especially by any youngster who has the good fortune to walk the woods and fields with one. This is partly because many of the shots the keeper takes on such occasions are comparatively easy, at going-away birds and beasts, and taken at fairly close range. But it is also due to the fact that by long experience he has become one with his gun, even if he was never fortunate enough to have it fitted to him. As Richard Jefferies wrote: 'It has become almost a portion of his body, answering like a limb to the volition of will without the intervention of reflection.' Time was, no doubt, when most keepers were good enough shots, in their limited sphere, but would have made a poor showing if they had had to deal with their own driven birds. Today this is less true, and the standard of shooting at gamekeepers' clay pigeon shoots is remarkably high. Those run each year by gunmakers Gallyon's of Norwich and Venables of Oxford are always well attended. Where a keeper is shooting as one of the Guns at a field trial, he can be depended on to keep the dogs occupied. He won't miss much. (Plate 22.)

The gamekeeper has no overtime; he gets a couple of weeks holiday a year, if he is lucky; his tips are taxed; he is underpaid and overworked; and he is the salt of the earth. A real individualist and one of nature's gentlemen, he is a countryman to whom no shooting man can talk for more than a few minutes without learning something interesting and probably quite fascinating. This is not, however, a treatise on how to be a keeper, even in an amateur way on one's own rough shoot, but rather a hint or two to the practical shooter about keepering matters on which he may be ignorant.

The host, the owner of the shoot, or the syndicate leader may organise much or little of a shooting day, but most of the detailed planning falls upon the keeper. He usually knows how the maximum number of birds may best be shown, and on the previous day he is out planting the numbered pegs for the Guns. He finds the beaters and stops and loaders, when required, and the pickers-up. On the day of the shoot, he is up and out on the ground two or three hours before the first drive, blanking-in spinneys and fields which hold birds, and pushing them into the main coverts. During the drive, his control of the beaters is the final essential towards success. At dusk on the day before, or very early that morning, he has lowered the wire netting ready at strategic places in the woods, and has set up the lines of small bits of coloured rag tied on to twine, called sewelling: these direct the pheasants the way he wants them to go and make them take wing instead of running to the edge of the wood and beyond. After the shoot, the sewelling must be taken away, for it is effective only when it suddenly confronts a bird in an unexpected place. The day after the shoot, even if it is a Sunday, sees the keeper and his dogs out on the ground again, searching for the birds which have not been picked-up. If collected at once, they can be added to the bag instead of being left to be eaten by scavengers.

How many Guns appreciate the skill and care that go into a successful pheasant drive? On the first one of a day in

[76]

November, when the early frosts have taken the leaves off
the trees, the birds clatter up through the bare branches
while they are still a hundred yards from the Guns and
make for another wood beyond. The sewelling is something
they do not like to run under. They fly over the trees, gain-
ing height, and cross the gun line thirty yards up or more.
'A marvellous stand!' the Guns say to each other after the
drive. 'Wonderful birds. Dam' difficult some of them,
weren't they?' It was not really the birds which were so
wonderful – it was that industrious keeper.

Later in the day, the covert which was behind the guns
on the first drive is taken. Besides its own stock of birds, it
contains those which escaped earlier. After plenty of shooting, the beaters halt fifty yards from the edge of the wood.
Wire netting has directed the birds forward, and stops on
the flanks have been tapping away with their sticks to prevent the birds from running out. The keeper walks slowly
forward alone and pushes up a few birds, first here and then
over there. Gently, he moves about while the silent beaters
tap with their sticks. For twenty minutes, there is an almost
continuous stream of birds over the valley where the Guns
have good and unflurried shooting. To an observer, with
time to notice what really goes on, it seems incredible –
especially when compared with the bad presentation sometimes seen on poorly run shoots.

At the end of the day, the keeper must pay the beaters
and see that the game is safely housed in his larder, after
distributions have been made to the Guns. If he is lucky, a
dealer will come and collect the game on the following day;
but if he has to pack it up himself and send it off by train
to the nearest city, he is in for a lot of extra work. The birds
have to be packed in hampers, taken to the railway station,
weighed and stacked on the platform. A hamper of twenty

[77]

pheasants is heavy, and the short-staffed country railway station probably cannot provide any help. The keeper may be able to sell some of his game to local shops or hotels, although this is yet another call on his time. Some dealers who accept game can be fussy about the condition of birds which have been badly shot, and they may also complain if the proportion of cocks and hens is not very nearly even. When the cheque comes in to the shoot, deductions have been made and the unpopular birds may be priced down to as little as £1 a brace. The keeper has no redress. The solution to the problem is to deal with a firm that offers an agreed price for all birds, taken as they come.

Selling the game is, of course, an important aspect of keeping down the cost of running a shoot, but not many of those who enjoy the shooting of it appreciate how much work may be involved in getting it to market. It is just another thing to bear in mind when you say goodbye to the keeper in the evening. Your thanks will be appreciated, together with a friendly comment on some aspect of the day – particularly if it has *not* been a very good day. When all goes well, everyone is happy; but when things are a little disappointing, perhaps due to atrocious weather, a little cheerful encouragement works wonders.

If in doubt about how much to tip the keeper, you should ask advice from your host. Some Guns are astonishingly mean in their tips, and some are vulgarly extravagant. Various scales have been suggested, according to the size of the shoot and the bag, but the amount of the tip should really take into account the efficiency and hard work of the keeper. You might, however, reflect on the declining value of money, which hits the keeper because of the convenience of the round sum of the pound note as a tip. If a day merited £5 in, say, 1975, the tip in 1981 ought to be £10 or more.

If it is a grouse or partridge shooting day the same basic principles apply, although nowadays the pheasant has become the mainstay of game shooting. As a result, pheasant rearing is one of the main aspects of shooting for sport which receives criticism from its opponents. Not that this concerns the keeper very much, but if you meet people who ask why pheasants cannot simply be bred like poultry and have their necks wrung when they are ready for eating, you might point out two main factors in the argument. One is that it is surely better to be born and enjoy some of the natural pleasures of a free life, as well as its fears and hurts, than never to have been born at all. The other point is that the preservation of any species, even for sport, undoubtedly conserves it, and without conservation many birds and animals would soon die out completely, killed by their natural enemies – predators, disease and unthinking men who consider them a nuisance.

Covert shooting which is carried out with hand-reared pheasants may be somewhat artificial, but the object should be to produce shooting of a high quality and not simply to make enormous bags. Wild pheasants, properly driven, can provide great sport; but when local circumstances do not favour a reasonable stock of wild birds, rearing is sensible and necessary. And reared birds, especially when driven back from a neighbouring covert to their home ground where they normally feed and sleep, can fly very well indeed, testing the skill of the best shots.

As is only to be expected, pheasant-rearing for sport has its opponents. Without going into the pros and cons of the arguments here, we should remember our debt to the British Field Sports Society, who are constantly upholding the interests of all field sports against their detractors. Our shoot preserves game – which means that the keeper controls the predators that try to kill it, and protects it from, and treats it for, the numerous diseases to which it is prone.

The keeper who rears pheasants will catch up the hens soon after Christmas and keep them in an open-topped aviary, with one wing brailed so that they cannot fly out. He may brail a few cocks, too, or just let free-flying cocks come in to 'tread' the hens. The alternative to brailing – in which the elbow joint of the wing is lightly bound with tape or, sometimes, a leather strap – is to clip the primary feathers of one wing. (Plate 29.) The advantage of clipping the wing is that the birds later release themselves, after the laying season, by growing new feathers. They do not have to be caught and handled. This is all right as long as their pen is situated near the centre of the shoot. But if it is near the edge, perhaps by the keeper's house alongside a road, he will probably prefer to brail his breeding pheasants and then take them to a central covert before releasing them. In this case, they will probably have to be penned for a short time while they recover full use of the brailed wing. Otherwise, they will walk back to the area of their old laying pen – and perhaps on, across the border. (Plate 35.)

The keeper collects the eggs in the spring and may hatch them under broody hens – which are becoming rare and expensive – or send them to a game farm for hatching. Or he may have an incubator – which is usually expensive and sometimes temperamental, needing careful watching. (Plate 30.) He can, alternatively, buy day-old chicks from a game farm, with or without broody hens. If broodies are not used, he will have brooders, usually powered by calor gas or paraffin, to keep the chicks warm. As they grow, the chicks have to be fed and watered, protected from cold and wet, moved into larger rearing pens, and then into release pens in the wood which is to be their home. Then they have to be encouraged to stay there, pushed back when they stray out, and fed continuously throughout the following shooting season. (Plate 31.)

All sorts of things can go wrong. Young pheasants appear to us to be remarkably silly. Sometimes they crowd together in a corner for warmth and suffocate each other; and there are many examples of their aptitude for self-destruction. For instance, during one of those summer thunderstorms which are apt to drench events like Ascot and Henley and Test matches, some of the pheasant chicks on a rearing field were in circular paraffin-heated brooders. The noise of the heavy rain and hail on the roof panicked them into swarming on top of each other. By the time the keeper reached the field to make sure they were not drowning outside the brooders, many of them were dead inside. Subsequently, he placed brushwood over the brooder roofs to deaden the sound of any further hailstones.

One of this keeper's friends had just put his poults into the release pen. Despite all the usual precautions, a fox got in one night and killed seventy-five of them within a space of about twenty yards. They were jugging on the ground, and presumably just waited to be slaughtered.

The heating arrangements of brooders are always susceptible to failure, whatever the method in use. One year the keeper met a new form of disaster when using a special paraffin lamp in a brooder. The chicks did well until they were about three weeks old, and then one night they evidently started stretching their wings. As they fluttered around, the lamp was partly extinguished. But it continued to smoulder, and then started to smoke. When the keeper had a look in the morning, he found a sad collection of little black bodies, all suffocated by the fumes.

Another evil which may befall him is to have his young

[81]

birds stolen from the rearing field. There are, unfortunately, those who, though they might not perform the actual theft themselves, are willing receivers, having let it be known in appropriate quarters that they are 'in the market'.

A brief explanation of only a few of the keeper's duties and problems should bring home to some of his shooting-day customers what he has to contend with on all the other days in the year. A visit to his rearing field during the summer would help to convince him that other people care about what goes on. And such a visit should be undertaken not as a duty but rather as a worthwhile interest. There is so much *more* to shooting than just the act of firing a gun.

The keeper wages constant war on vermin, and his traps are inspected every day. He must guard against poachers – the simple and artless as well as the organised gangs who may strip a covert the day before a shoot. He has to compete with agricultural hazards which include grubbing out hedges to make larger, more economical fields and the use of chemical sprays often injurious to the insects and seeds on which his birds could thrive. He must keep a count of the birds on his beat, which means examining the ground for pairing partridges in March and watching the progress of their broods in August.

On a grouse moor, he will be organising the rotation of heather burning during winter and early spring in order to produce succulent new shoots on which the birds will feed. And as August 12th approaches, he will be observing with special care the numbers of birds on his moor. Keepers are naturally reluctant to predict the numbers of birds they have, but this is an essential part of game management. Assessing the stock before shooting begins is vital if the correct bag is to be taken subsequently, because shooting should be proportional to breeding production. Many birds will die during the winter, anyway; and if breeding conditions are not sufficiently good a policy of sparing the birds in the autumn is uneconomic.

The keeper should be able to combine tact with firmness in his dealings with tenant farmers and their workers as well as with foresters, neighbouring keepers and the local Hunt. He has to be alert at all times to what is happening on the whole of his beat. If he concentrates too much on preparing his rearing field and neglects to have a look round other places, he may find that a tenant farmer, who when approached is always prepared to co-operate, has decided to indulge in a spate of mechanical hedge-trimming just when and where the partridges are nesting and hatching.

The keeper does not welcome many modern farming methods but he has to live with them – and indeed, coping with them successfully is one of his main tasks. Like all sportsmen, he regrets the decline of the partridge; and one of his theories about this decline centres upon myxomatosis. He says the rabbits used to graze the grass and corn near the hedges so that it was very short; now that it grows higher, no longer nibbled by rabbits, the insects on it are too high up for young partridges to reach. So a source of food for them is removed – like the seeds of weeds killed by sprays, and the loss of the gleanings in stubble fields burnt immediately after harvest. He remembers how, before the coming of chemical sprays, there were anthills on the rough ground bordering the fields; now the sprays drift across and kill the ants, once a popular food for his partridges and wild pheasants. Ants used to be a major nutritional part of a partridge chick's food, and a correct diet is vital if the bird is to survive the effects of cold, wet and disease. Myxomatosis can also be blamed for the decline in the numbers of ants. Anthills require warmth to allow the pupae they contain to develop; but without grazing rabbits, long grass and brambles grow over the antills, shading them from the sun and preventing continued breeding of ants.

The keeper must find the nests of his wild birds in the spring, guard them from predators, and probably collect some of the eggs to be hatched with those he is rearing. He is a handy man at carpentry when a pen needs repairing or a crow trap has to be made. In fact, he has a vast number of jobs calling for his attention all the year round, and many of them involve battling against something which is trying to defeat *him*. (Plate 32.) A right-of-way through his woods can be a constant source of worry. Innocent walkers may happily enjoy the primroses and bluebells, but some of them have wild dogs which roam far from the paths and kill his nesting birds. Some of the walkers are not so innocent; they bear some sort of a misguided grudge against him and all that he stands for. They delight in seeking out his traps and either springing or stealing them. Foul weather; a poaching cat; game bird diseases like gapes, aspergillosis, moniliasis and coccidiosis – all threaten death to his charges.

When the villagers see him working in his garden during a summer afternoon they think he is a lucky chap, being able to garden whenever he wants to. But they probably don't know that he was up at five in the morning and will be out in the coverts at ten o'clock in the evening. Perhaps there has been a fox somewhere near his young birds, and he may have to stay up all night to get it. He uses Renardine around his release pen in the wood, and sometimes he threads small tins containing pebbles on to a nylon line fixed about eight inches off the ground; a fox cannot see the nylon, but when it bumps into it the tins rattle frighteningly. There are times, however, when a marauding fox has to be shot, even though the shoot is on good terms with the Hunt.

If the shoot is to be successful, the keeper's relations with his employer must be good – and they usually are. The lucky keeper has a fairly free hand, with the boss taking an interest but inevitably watching the costs. The keeper likes to see mangolds and swedes and sugar beet in the fields, and not acres and acres of corn which will be ploughed as soon as they are harvested. He particularly wants to see some kale, and a crop dear to his heart is kale planted with strips of barley down the middle. The combine-harvester can run down each strip, and the stubble and the kale is left until the end of the shooting season. This is a certain draw for birds. In flat country where it is difficult to show high pheasants, the keeper will drive the birds out of the nearby woods into the kale. Then he will take the beaters through the kale, away from the wood and the line of Guns. As the birds fly back over the beaters to their home covert, they are fast and difficult targets. It may be, however, that the keeper will be unable to persuade the boss on the home farm, or any of the tenant farmers, to plant a few crops in a manner helpful to the shoot – in which case, he must just battle on as best he can.

He may have a struggle persuading his employer to pay sufficiently high wages. Beaters were paid £7 a day in 1980, and pickers-up £8. Stops who are out on the ground at dawn earn a little more; and all those tractor drivers and woodmen who, in the spring, report when they find nests are worth some reward. If the keeper is unable to make adequate payments, the shoot will suffer.

Not all keepers are paragons. Some are lazy and useless. The good ones should not be interfered with unduly: but they should also not be left to worry alone when things go wrong.

The successful gamekeeper is a diplomat and a disciplinarian. He has to be dedicated to his job. Gamekeeping is certainly not for an idle youngster who expects to do little more than wander round the fields and woods with a gun under his arm, despite the fact that some people might think so. For instance, only last season, a Gun was heard to remark to a keeper: 'That was a marvellous day, Harry. You've certainly worked hard. But what on earth do you find to do in the summer?'

CHAPTER FIVE

ROUGH SHOOTING, DOGS AND SAFETY

FRANK used to do a bit of deer stalking and rough shooting on Haldon, in the West Country. One day, he was shooting pigeons and rabbits with a 12-bore when he came suddenly upon a stag standing at the top of a bank about twenty-five yards away. He took a quick shot and bowled it over, apparently dead. He ran forward to bleed the animal; but as he bent down, it jumped up. He flung his arms round its neck to try to drag it down. They wrestled, rolling over and over down the bank, and the knife was knocked from Frank's hand. The deer was kicking frantically. Finally, Frank had to let go, and it bounded up and away. Considerably shaken, Frank stood up and found that, as well as several nasty cuts and bruises, he had suffered the loss of his corduroy breeches. From his waist belt to the laced part of the breeches below his knees, there remained nothing but a couple of tattered strips.

Not all rough shooting is quite as rough as this . . .

Incidentally, it is now illegal to shoot deer with a shotgun loaded with cartridges containing pellets smaller than SSG.

Rough shooting generally implies informality – walking-up with dogs and, where any driving takes place, the Guns usually taking turns to act as beaters. A rough shoot does not normally have a full-time keeper to look after it, although it certainly needs some amateur keepering – even if this is no more than constant visits throughout the year by the owners of the shooting rights. There are three character-istics about the rough shoot: it is what nearly all shooting men would like to have; it needs sufficient dogs if the bag is to be at all commensurate with the potential of the ground; and it is the scene of an alarming amount of dangerous behaviour.

Finding a rough shoot requires diligent searching and an ear to the ground, with visits to farmers, landowners, game-keepers and estate agents. The sporting papers occasionally carry advertisements for shoots, and Forestry Commission ground is sometimes leased by tender. When shooting rights are rented, it is important that a correct form of contract is drawn up. A couple of signatures on a vaguely-worded piece of paper, or simply a 'gentleman's agreement' about the rent, can lead to misunderstanding and much disappoint-ment later on. A document suitable for this type of contract can be obtained from *Shooting Times and Country Magazine*, address in Appendix D.

Since it is difficult to obtain shooting rights, one may have to accept almost anything that is offered. But in case there is a choice, a few points are worth considering. Anything less than about 300 acres is scarcely worth while, unless it is very well positioned. The area should be more or less circular rather than a long thin strip. A main road running through the middle is a considerable disadvantage, and the nature of the surrounding land is important – urban or country, keepered or wild. A good bet is a piece of land well into the country, away from easy access for poachers from towns, farmed by or adjoining the land of a sympathetic farmer, containing some woodland, preferably facing south and not entirely open and exposed to north winds.

Rough shooting used to be thought of as a sport for one or

two friends renting the rights, quite cheaply, on a small piece of land where they could walk around with a gun whenever they felt like it. This still applies for some lucky people: but more often the modern rough shoot – owing to the scarcity of suitable land and the increasing number of would-be shooters – costs more money and warrants more care and looking after. And so more friends join together to help pay the cost and do the work. Having taken action to control predators, and having enjoyed any 'free' shooting, such as the odd pheasant and any pigeon which use the area, they set about improving the shoot.

Just as the farmer's footprint is supposed to be the best manure for the farm, so the presence of one of the Guns is the greatest benefit to a rough shoot which is being improved. If it is left fallow too long, it will suffer from the attentions of four-legged, winged and two-legged predators. Some sort of rearing of game birds is bound to be attempted, or at least poults will be bought to be released around August. Hoppers of corn will be placed in the coverts, and perhaps ambitious attempts will be made to encourage duck by creating flight ponds. Mechanical digging is expensive, but manpower can be used to dam streams. In marshy ground, explosive charges can be employed to form a network of small pools. The booklets issued by The Game Conservancy, Fordingbridge, Hampshire, on all aspects of shoot management are excellent. Some which would be particularly helpful on a rough shoot are: *Pheasant Rearing, Winter Feeding and Management, Wildfowl on Inland Waters, Winged Vermin Control, Control of Ground Predators,* and *Game on the Farm.*

On taking over a rough shoot, the first task, nearly always, is to deal with predators – or carry on the good work if the shoot has been cared for previously. Rearing pheasants or

[89]

putting down poults in the late summer is wasted effort unless the numbers of their predatory enemies are kept under control. These enemies of game are mainly stoats, weasels, rats, grey squirrels, foxes, crows, jays, magpies, and domestic cats gone wild. All of these may be shot or trapped, but traps must be visited daily. Incidentally, in a tunnel trap for small marauders the 'Fenn' trap seems to be the most popular with professional keepers. When Warfarin is put down for rats, it must be continued until they stop eating it if it is to be properly effective.

Rearing can be done on a small scale at home, especially if the members of the shoot keep a few chickens. Game farms supply pheasant eggs, but it is usually a better bargain to buy day-old chicks at about twice the price of eggs. The farms will also supply adult birds from their own laying pens by June, and these will probably still lay a few more eggs. They are cheaper than poults, which are birds of the year. Before poults are released, they should be kept in a fox-proof pen; and at this time a daily visit by a member of the shoot is essential, to check that all is well and to replenish food and water supplies. Messrs. Gilbertson and Page of Hertford, Hertfordshire, in conjunction with the Cotswold Game Farm, can supply practically everything needed on a shoot: eggs, birds, food, pens, snares, traps and medicines, etc.

Much of the actual shooting on a rough shoot is done when walking-up. The first essential, in order to hit the target, is that the shooter should stop walking and adopt a steady stance before he tries to put up his gun. You must not bring up the gun as the left foot comes to the ground, and still less must you try to shoot with the right foot in front of the left. Place your left foot firmly on the ground towards the bird, which is at 12 o'clock, with the toes pointing at

1 o'clock, body leaning slightly forward so that most of the weight is on the left leg; the right foot should be about eight inches behind the left, toes pointing at 3 o'clock, heel just off the ground (see Figure 1). You then, with the left hand, push the muzzles along the line of flight of the bird and mount the gun as described in Chapter One.

There should be no undue hurry about the movement of raising the butt and firing. It must all be done with rhythm and smoothness, culminating in a squeeze of the trigger without any snatch. There may often be a tendency to shoot too soon, particularly at a pheasant which suddenly jumps up almost at one's feet. This target is absurdly easy to miss, with both barrels, the shot going harmlessly under the bird's tail. Watch the bird's head and, after the first burst of acceleration, follow it with your muzzles as it settles into a steady flight, swing through it and knock it down at twenty or thirty yards, instead of letting your excitement cause you to miss it at ten yards. Take your time and 'read' the line of flight. With the muzzles kept steadily along it, you will have achieved seventy-five per cent of your task before ever you mount the gun to your shoulder.

It may seem obvious to say that one must stop walking before taking a shot, but it is so important to get one's stance correct and people do try to shoot with their feet in most awkward positions. Correct footwork puts the body in the right position and enhances one's ability to keep the swing going.

Rough shooting means that hares and rabbits will have to be dealt with. When you are thus shooting downwards, *bend* forward from the hips. The rest of the stance remains the same, but you should not stand firmly upright and merely poke the barrels down. If a hare is crossing your front, you should place your left foot not *at* the hare but approximately where it will be when you are going to shoot it. So just before picking up the animal over your muzzles, more or less in front of you, your left foot should move across about ten inches in the direction in which the hare is going. As the hare runs on, your swing is comfortably over your left foot and can be continued easily, even if you need to fire the second barrel. This drill of moving the left foot before the gun is mounted, pivoting on the ball of the right foot, can be applied to any moving target.

Sometimes, across a narrow ride or in a gap between trees, someone brings off what is termed a 'snap' shot: a very quick bit of work which pleases him and probably invokes congratulations from onlookers. It is thought of as aiming at where the target is expected to be in a split second, but without proper preparation for the shot. The shooter thinks there is no time to swing, and so the gun is just flung up and fired in front of the bird or rabbit. Doing this *may* bring success, but it is not the correct way. In fact, it is rarely done. The so-called snapshot is normally only a quick shot done in the orthodox manner.

If an indifferent performer brings off a snap shot, there is a danger that he may think he has found a short cut to success. If he tries his technique of 'aiming where the bird is going to be' on a normal shot, when he has plenty of time, he will almost certainly poke at the bird and miss. If you are pleased with a snap shot, remember that all you did was to perform a well-placed quick shot. For other normal shots, when you have plenty of time you can do equally well. The technique of shooting driven birds is dealt with fully in *Shotgun Marksmanship*.

Dogs are almost as essential to shooting as guns. Indeed, some sportsmen consider that to go out without a dog is to be only half equipped and that, very often, more satisfaction can be obtained with a dog and no gun than with a gun and no dog. On a rough shoot, a dog becomes particularly important because of the 'shortage of staff'. Any keen dog is better than none to flush game from thick cover like brambles and kale, but naturally a reasonably biddable one is preferable. Terriers, dachshunds and nondescripts can all help; and poodles sometimes make good shooting dogs, too. Dachshunds not over-bred for show purposes often have very good noses and will tell you for sure if there is a rabbit down a hole or a rat under some logs. (Plate 36.)

If you are going to form a little rough-shooting club, with the members sharing the rent and the upkeep and the work, it really is essential that there should be some dogs among the shooters. With a big syndicate for more formal shooting this is less essential because there is more money to pay the staff which will include a proper complement of beaters and pickers-up. (Plates 33, 39.)

Not everyone is in a position to keep a gundog. Many keen, eager to learn, and even quite knowledgeable gun owners live in cities and have neither time nor space. They enjoy their shooting days tremendously, and it would be no bad thing if some of them would think a little about how much of their enjoyment they owe to their companions who do keep a dog. It is all too easy for a non-dog-owner to criticise the efforts made by a friend who is trying to work his dog. The following is a typical example of what happens:

Charlie has knocked down a runner, and Philip brings over his dog to look for it. 'Hi, lost!' says Philip, indicating the line given him by Charlie, and the dog quests eagerly across the field. The pheasant appears a hundred yards ahead and scuttles across to the right, making for a small spinney. The dog overshoots the place where the pheasant

[93]

had squatted, works back, picks up the line and follows on. It is now a few yards from the bird and has its nose down, puzzling out this line on a frosty day with precious little scent. Charlie, with his eyes at about five-foot six inches from ground level, thinks the dog is 'a bit of a damned fool' if it can't see 'that ruddy great pheasant' only a few yards in front of it. He takes no account of the fact that the dog's eyes are only about three or four inches above the ground and that, in any case, its concentration is entirely in the almost miraculous sensitivity of its nose. Finally, the dog comes up to within about a yard of the pheasant, sees it, picks it up and comes galloping back. 'Thanks,' says Charlie when Philip hands over his bird; but he thinks that he might have nabbed it more quickly if he had run after it himself. He may simply not be aware of the fact that all those other birds of his which had been picked-up over the years, in thick cover and far away at the back end of various woods, were added to the bag because somebody else's dog used its nose, without interference or criticism. Truly, the dogless shooter rarely has just reason for speaking or even thinking unkindly of a companion whose dog is almost bound to contribute some good.

Sometimes, however, there is justification for harsh thoughts, as in the case of the dog which remains tethered to its master for much of the time – contributing nothing to the finding of unshot game – and which, when let off its lead, runs around mouthing birds lying in the open and so helping not at all in the pick-up. There was a cocker-spaniel bitch who belonged in this category. One day, the Guns on a rough shoot were enjoying their lunch in the October sunshine, with the modest bag of a dozen or so head laid out on the grass. The bitch kept sniffing at the birds and pushing them around, for which she was rather ineffectually admonished by her master. After lunch, the cocker and one partridge were missing. Some time later, master and bitch were reunited – but the partridge was never found. That was a day when one spaniel's contribution to the bag was plus nothing and definitely minus one.

The most common way of getting a gundog is to buy a pup as soon as it is weaned. This is reasonable if the new owner has plenty of time for training and enough room in the way of a large garden or nearby open country. It is the cheapest way to buy a dog but not the surest way of getting a suitable one. Trying to select the right pup from a litter which is only about seven weeks old is much more difficult than is generally realised. The advantages of buying a youngster of between six and nine months with very little training, and before it has learnt any faults, are that you can see the 'shape' of the adult dog and its probable inherent characteristics, some of which may be very difficult to change: features such as boldness, willingness, a natural desire to retrieve and carry things, car-sickness, gun-shyness, timidity or a tendency to fight. It will also be ready at that age to start its serious training.

At about nine weeks old, a pup must have its initial vaccination – to be followed by a booster dose   against distemper, hardpad, contagious hepatitis, leptospira, canicola and leptospira icterohaemorrhagiae. The last is a form of jaundice transmitted by rats or the urine of infected dogs, and it can be lethal. It can also be passed on to humans.

Some people make their start by acquiring a dog of about a couple of years old – 'going cheap to good home'. It is virtually untrained, but as it is a gundog breed the new owner has high hopes when he takes it along to his rough shoot. There the animal has a great time –

tearing around, flushing game, sometimes carrying a bird because that is in its blood, but never retrieving to hand, running-in to shot and chasing every rabbit and hare that appears. The owner feels disappointed and wonders what he should do to make his dog behave better. He has made the common error of taking the dog shooting too soon, without any preliminary training. The only cure is to go right back to initial discipline and obedience training, and not take the dog near any shooting until this has been put right. The owner is unlikely to have the facilities for such training, which must be very thorough and include work in a rabbit pen; and even if he sends the dog to a professional trainer there can be no certainty that the dog's temperament will permit it to be cured of its faults. Training out bad habits is always far more difficult than teaching good behaviour to raw material. The choice for this owner is either to retain his keen and wild dog, which may be useful for wildfowling and may, or may not, be accepted on the rough shoot for its one or two slight assets, or – if he really wants an obedient and steady dog – to cut his losses and begin again with a younger animal which has not had the opportunity of learning the ways of wickedness.

Another way of obtaining a gundog is to buy one of about a year or eighteen months old which has already been trained professionally. This could cost anything from £200 to £400. The new owner must carry on the training, at least as far as insisting that discipline learnt is not allowed to lapse. A good dog can easily be spoiled by a poor handler, and it is generally true to say that there are far more bad handlers than bad dogs. While it is still young, even a well-trained dog lacks experience in the shooting field, and the owner must to some extent sublimate his shooting to furthering the education of his dog. Unless the young dog is con-

A Pheasant over the Valley

37. A stylish shot although not a very high bird

A Pheasant in the Wood

38. It is curling away to the left; he seems to have swung in front all right, but it wo
have been better if he had moved his left foot round before he put the gun up. The
looks steady.

A MIXED BAG

39. From a useful little rough shoot bordering an estuary: pheasant, partridge, mallard, wigeon, curlew and a hare.

A DRINK FOR THE DOG

40. From its master's hands cupped under neck of a bottle of water; after a warm afternoon's pigeon shooting in August.

'WARE WIRE

41. A good leap over pig wire by a young labrador, carrying a French partridge. The strand of barbed wire sometimes found at the top of the fence is a danger to dogs, especially those who do not jump boldly, as a scramble over the top can result in nasty injuries.

DOGS DURING LUNCH

42. It may be unwise to leave dogs loose outside while their owners are having lunch. It is certainly foolish to leave guns leaning against the wall.

Dangerous Muzzles

43 They point at dogs and other men's feet. The guns are probably unloaded but no one knows for certain.

Thoughtless Behaviour

44. Carefree he sits on his shooting stick, gun across his knees, a danger to his neighbour or anyone who passes by.

WHICH WAY WILL THE BIRDS FLIGHT?

45. The fowler's eternal question as he looks out over the mud of the estuary.

WILDFOWLER'S HIDE

46. He is sitting on his game bag with his feet in a hole, behind an old oil drum and a piece of sacking hung on the fence. If he leans forward and puts the dog on his right they will both be well hidden. With snow on the ground some fowlers drape a white sheet over themselves.

A PULL-THROUGH

47. Carried in the pocket, it may save the day if the **barrels**
become choked with mud or snow.

A SWIVEL SEAT

48. The bottom plate is big enough not to sink in mud and the top swivels
horizontally and a little vertically. The shooter, squatting behind cover, can
take a shot from a sitting position in any direction.

GOOSE DECOYS

49. These are on the sand of an estuary. They would be more effective on an inland field, although such use is often considered unsporting.

DUCK DECOYS

50. These are self-inflating rubber ones, light and easily carried. The dog is being introduced to them so that it will learn not to retrieve one instead of a real bird.

stantly under the eye of its master, it will quickly become unsteady and regard a shooting day as primarily designed for *its* enjoyment – especially if it is in the company of other undisciplined dogs. Bad habits are, unfortunately, easier to pick up than good ones. Although the atmosphere of a rough shoot is more easy-going than that of a formal shoot, it is a great mistake to take out an animal whose obedience training is incomplete, or one which is an expensively trained new acquisition, and think that you can concentrate on shooting and ignore the dog.

As regards training one's own gun-dog, it is most advisable to read a book by an acknowledged master on the subject (see Appendix 'J'). Meanwhile, here are a few points which may help the amateur trainer.

The dog need not be kept in an outside kennel. The belief that it should lingers on from the days when almost everyone who shot lived in the country and had plenty of outhouses and stables, and gundogs were never allowed in the house. A gundog can be a pet, but not a pampered one. It does not need to be fed on chocolates and the best steaks; and it should not be taken for walks by irresponsible children who may encourage it to chase rabbits. But it *can* live in the house with the family without coming to any harm. Indeed, that desirable confidence between master and dog can be built up by the two being together as much as possible. And obedience training, especially in the early stages, can be continued during normal activities around the home – whether it is learning to 'Sit' while you help with the washing-up or 'Heel' while you walk round the garden.

Unless you have a large garden, you will want access to some open space. A public park has the disadvantage of other dog-smells, so it is best to use a field in the country.

[97]

To get there, you might consider bicycling – with the dog on a long cord – in order to save time if you have to fit in the training period before going to work in the morning or after returning in the evening.

As part of normal house-training, it is a great help if you always take the pup to the same place in the garden to relieve itself. This can be a rough corner, perhaps behind the garage or otherwise out of sight, and the pup should soon come to associate the situation with the action required. If you have a bitch, this is especially useful when it grows older and uses its lavatory by choice instead of wetting the lawn and killing the grass.

After learning to answer its name, the dog must be taught to come to the whistle, blown in several short blasts. Having learned to walk to heel and to sit, it can be taught 'Down', meaning 'Lie down' from the sitting position. This may be useful months ahead when you are crouching in a gutter as duck approach; and the initial teaching prevents the dog from begging at mealtimes or generally making a nuisance of itself when visitors come to the house. Professional teachers often use the word 'Hup' to make a dog sit. This paradoxical-sounding word may have originated as an abbreviation of the cry 'muzzles up', used in the time of muzzle-loaders when a halt was called to recharge the gun. Amateurs may prefer to use 'Sit', and use 'Up' for telling the dog to jump up into a car.

A word any pup will quickly be interested in is 'Dinner'. Gentle discipline training can be extended into feeding time by sitting the dog, placing the food bowl some distance away, and letting it go to its meal only on the order 'Dinner'. This, of course, is training for a youngster of six to nine months or so, not a helpless little two-months-old puppy. It is not a bad thing to teach the word 'Water', too, by indicating the bowl when the dog is thirsty. Later, when you are out shooting on a hot day – perhaps after the pigeon at harvest time – and you see a water trough, you can send the dog to get a drink. This can save you having to climb through the fence and take the dog to the water.

It is most important that a dog can be left in a car without doing damage. After it has passed the puppy stage of chewing almost everything, put it in the car and then return to the house and watch through a window. When the pup starts jumping from one seat to the other, scratching at the window, or chewing your hat, you can go out and scold it. The animal is only bored and restless, and it has not yet achieved that state of confidence in you which tells it that everything is really all right and that you will be back before long. If the dog starts howling and barking, you will need much patience and perseverance to make it stay put quietly. But a dog which cannot be left in house or car can be very vexing indeed. In extreme cases, it may have to be discarded as a shooting dog.

One of the first words the pup must learn is 'No', used for all manner of misdeeds. This can be followed up with a scolding. As training progresses, the word should be sufficient by itself to stop the animal from doing almost anything. Beating is never necessary and is, in any case, very difficult to administer without losing one's temper. If you want to chastise the dog, act like the leader of the pack: get hold of it by the loose skin of the throat (in your hand; no need to use your teeth!) and shake it.

Perhaps the most useful achievement in obedience training is to get the dog to answer to the stop whistle. One blast, and it stops and sits. It stops chasing something it shouldn't; it looks for directions towards what it is supposed to be finding; or it simply stops – and thereby avoids being run over

[99]

when you are walking along a country road and a car suddenly appears. The basic answer to the question 'How do I train my dog?' is that you just *do*. Go on repeating – but in small doses so that the pupil does not become bored – and reward it with love and maybe a tit-bit whenever it does something right. All dog training is *habit* training.

When introduced to water, the pup will probably enjoy frolicking about in the shallows but may be disinclined to go out of its depth and swim. To overcome this, do not push it into deep water but put on a pair of thigh boots and wade out yourself, encouraging the pupil to follow. It soon will. If it doesn't, the fault is yours. Wait until there is more confidence between the two of you and try again.

The dummy used to teach retrieving can take several forms. Those used at working tests are often covered with canvas and cannot be very attractive to a dog, and one may be inclined to wonder at the sagacity of the dog in knowing that so dull an object really is what it is looking for. In the earliest stages, a puppy can be encouraged to carry a rolled-up sock, or glove, or handkerchief – or, indeed, almost anything. When a proper dummy is required, one which can be thrown and will float, a good one can be made from a small log of wood wrapped round with clean rag and covered with an old sock tied at the end. *After* the pupil has encountered game, you can tuck in under the sock a few outer-wing joints from pheasants, cut off when you are plucking them. This gives the dummy a scent, which is helpful when sending the pupil on long distance blind retrieves and practising hand signals. These signals represent fairly advanced training, but they are not just 'fancy stuff' only needed at field trials. A dog that answers to hand signals is most useful when a bird is dropped across water – when wildfowling, for instance; and when pigeon-shooting from a hide where it cannot see the fall and may, in any case, need to be directed away from disturbing the decoys.

What breed is most suitable for the rough shooter? And should it be a dog or a bitch? The pros and cons can occupy many an evening's glass-in-hand argument and provide much free copy for the 'Letters to the Editor' page of the sporting magazines. Probably the best answer to the breed question is springer spaniel; and all owners of bitches are quite sure that in the long run they are less trouble than dogs. Although they have their periods in season, bitches are otherwise far less likely to wander from home; they rarely fight; and they do not have that tiresome urge to leave their visiting cards on your friends' property. On the other hand, they ought to be allowed at least one family of pups – and you may not have adequate facilities for looking after these. If you are thinking of making money from occasional breeding, you should remember that a good dog can earn stud fees with far less trouble to its owner.

Springers are wonderful hunting dogs, and when properly trained they are a joy to behold. But they are not easy for an amateur to train. He would probably find a labrador more amenable to discipline.

As long as the chosen dog comes from working stock, it should respond to training; but there are occasional misfits who simply will not happily pick up the dummy. Professional trainers sometimes employ forced retrieving, but it is a sad business. If you are unlucky enough to have a dog which does not enjoy retrieving, you had better start again and get another one.

You will have to trust to luck with regard to your animal's intelligence. Dogs often tend to be brighter than bitches in that they are more wilful and tend to think things out for themselves and perhaps act as *they* think best – which is not

[101]

always the same as their master thinks. For example, a party was once shooting partridges over downland bordering the sea and two birds dropped over the cliff on to the beach. It was not a very high cliff and there was a narrow, awkward path down it which a dog might manage. Two or three dogs were sent for the birds, but they all refused to go more than a few yards down the steep path. Finally, old Nero – the apple of his master's eye, steady as a rock and full of years and experience – was told the situation. He ambled off down the path, cautiously and cleverly, reached the beach and found the two partridges lying within a yard or two of each other. He picked up one and moved over to the other. All the Guns watched expectantly from the cliff-top. Nero went to pick up the second bird, muffed it a bit and dropped the first one. He tried again. Two birds were too much of a mouthful. He eyed the cliff and that tricky little path. Maybe he thought 'Damned if I'm going up and down there twice.' But what to do? He picked up one bird, pondered a moment, put it down and picked up the second one. That, too, he put down. Then he solemnly lay down and solved his problem by eating one of the birds. When the last bit had gone, he picked up the remaining partridge, carefully climbed up the cliff path and presented it majestically to his master. Intelligent? Wilful? No man can know all that goes on in a dog's mind, but the episode was the highlight of that day's shooting.

Of course, some sagacious dogs will carry two birds at once. One dog is on record as having put down, and held with his paw, a wounded bird he was retrieving while he picked up a dead bird; he then gathered the runner as well and returned with the two. An even more clever feat concerned a labrador which lifted out of its form a half-grown hare just as a nearby Gun shot a pheasant, which ran; the dog, still carrying the leveret, went after the bird and soon returned carrying them both, each looking out of opposite sides of its mouth.

An unusual retrieve concerned a vanished partridge. It was seen to fall into an overgrown ditch but the dogs could make nothing of it, until the owner of a flatcoat retriever sent in his bitch. She hunted around for several minutes and then came out carrying an old iron kettle by its handle; inside was the still alive partridge. But we digress from discussing the choice of breed.

The labrador has much to commend it as the choice of the shooting man who is his own trainer. Not all owners know that the breed came, not from Labrador, but from Newfoundland. It was originally the St. John's water-dog; but it was referred to as a labrador when it was imported, in order to distinguish it from the larger and shaggier-coated Newfoundland dog. The breed was first brought to England by salmon-boat crews returning from Newfoundland to Poole harbour in about 1830. It had been used by cod-fishermen off Newfoundland to retrieve fish that escaped from the hook as they were being pulled in; hence its remarkably water repellent coat. Not all labradors die young, as some people suppose; there was one working around recently which was eighteen years old. When bred from working stock, labradors have a wonderful instinct for retrieving. It is not unknown for a pup of about two months to pick up a dead bird — or even an egg – in the garden and carry it, instead of chewing it as most breeds would.

You will hear stories of proud owners who have taken their young dogs out with a gun, usually to the effect that 'He retrieved a cock pheasant first time – a runner, too! And he's only six months old.' It cannot be emphasised too strongly that the tendency to try to run before one can

[103]

walk must be resisted. It is very natural to want to see how a pup will get on with the real thing; but a too hasty introduction can, in a few minutes, undo weeks and months of training. And nowhere is this more likely to happen than in the company of cheerfully undisciplined animals on a rough shoot!

It should be self-evident that the dog's well-being is his owner's first duty after shooting, taking precedence over cleaning the gun and certainly over having a drink.

Carry a bottle of water in the car, especially during hot weather and when wildfowling, where the dog encounters salt water. (Plate 40.) After the shoot, dry the dog underneath, at least partially, using newspaper; but do not rub too hard along its back because that merely rubs the wet into its protective undercoat. A chamois leather is better than an old towel, but newspaper is a very good spare to carry in the car; it is also useful to absorb dampness between the dog and the sacking or rug on which it lies for the journey home.

A nasty hazard which gundogs have to face is barbed wire, particularly that one strand which often tops the square plain wire enclosing pens. Many dogs are courageous enough in jumping this obstacle, clear or feet-on-and-feet-off like a hunter over a West Country bank (Plate 41), but a slip on the barbed wire can cause a nasty wound in the guts. An immediate visit to a vet is essential in the case of a wound serious enough to need stitching, but one safeguard is to carry some Aureomycin powder in the car to put on such a wound in the meantime.

The cost of visits to a vet, food, and kennels when you are on holiday is not inconsiderable, but is absolutely worth it to have a dog to share and increase your pleasure in shooting. Food bills need not be excessive if you buy wisely and get meat from an abattoir: and tripe, though smelly, is cheap and nutritional. Nearly all pet dogs are overfed. Professional dog-trainers often fast their trainees one day a week, with entirely beneficial results.

Do not carry a dog in the boot of a car, even with the lid propped open a bit. If it does not die from carbon-monoxide poisoning, it will certainly suffer – and so will its scenting powers.

Earlier in this chapter, reference was made to dangerous behaviour. Though this is not confined to the rough shoot, certain of the more outrageous examples occur on some rough shoots because of the inexperience of a few of the Guns. Safety is a perennial subject in shooting lore, and dreadful examples of what happens when the rules are ignored appear continually in the press. Much of what follows applies wherever guns are used – whether on a formal shoot, by a wildfowler on his own, or by a group of friends walking-up a bit of rough stuff. The particular bearing on rough shooting is that, because of the probable shortage of game, there is a great tendency for everyone to try a shot at practically any chance in order to have something in the bag. This way lies danger through irresponsible behaviour.

The other source of danger is the condition of the weapon itself. One day, at a farmers' shoot, the guests crowded into the back of a Land-Rover after the first drive and the host offered old Fred the front passenger seat. It was an early-type car with a canvas roof. As Fred sat down, he plonked the butt of his gun down on the floor with the barrels pointing up vertically between his knees. As he did so the gun went off and blew a hole through the roof. No one spoke for a moment, and then old Fred said: 'Dang me if the same thing didn't happen last week!'

Some of the faults often present in old and neglected guns were mentioned in Chapter Two. Note that on all but the very best sidelock guns the safety-catch does no more than lock the triggers. In a worn gun, the bent can slip off the nose of the sear if the weapon is propped against something and then falls over, or if it is jarred like old Fred's (Fig. II). No closed gun is ever 'safe'. The only way you can check this is to open it and have a look.

If you have a misfire, lower the gun so that the muzzles point to the ground, put on the safety-catch and open the gun. When you have removed the cartridge, look up the barrels before reloading. It sometimes happens that the cap fires and the powder does not. It is even possible that the powder charge may have been omitted through faulty loading. The small explosion of the cap could be sufficient to force the shot and wads a short way into the barrel, where the wadding would cause an obstruction. If another cartridge is then hurriedly loaded, the next shot will probably burst the barrel and injure the shooter.

Another cause of a misfire could be the inadvertent loading of a smaller bore cartridge. A 20-bore cartridge will slip through the chamber of a 12-bore gun and lodge in the barrels. If the shooter omits to look up the barrels after a misfire of this nature and loads a 12-bore cartridge, a burst will surely follow. Cartridges should always be most carefully segregated according to size. Some accident-wise shooting men will not allow 20-bore and 12-bore cartridges to be kept in the same room, or even the same house.

Guns should always be unloaded before crossing a ditch or a fence, or before putting them in a car or bringing them into a building. If you are carrying an unloaded gun and you reach a fence, break the gun to ensure that it is un-

loaded before you clamber over; and make a similar check
before putting it in the car. You may *know* you unloaded it
a few minutes before, but there is nothing to be lost in
making assurance doubly sure. Many accidents are caused
by allegedly unloaded guns. Someone once said that the two
most dangerous things on a farm are a quiet bull and an
unloaded gun.

Safe gun-handling ought to be a drill which becomes
automatic, so that the first thing you do when you pick up a
gun is open it to make sure it is not loaded. Most of us,
fortunately, have not witnessed a serious accident and so we
forget that any gun is always a potentially dangerous
weapon. It should be impossible for a shooting man to
pass his gun to a friend to have a look at, for instance,
without breaking it to show that it is unloaded. But this sort
of thing is happening somewhere every day – an example of
thoughtless behaviour which may be a prelude to one of
those salutary reports we see of people who pull a gun
towards them, muzzles first, through a hedge or out of a car.

Regarding behaviour while actually shooting, we all know
that we are not supposed to swing across the line of guns –
but accidents still happen due to this sin, committed in the
excitement of the moment. It is remarkable, however, that
more casualties are not caused by shooting where the man
with the gun *can't* see where his shot is going. Never shoot
if you are uncertain whether anyone is in the line of fire.
This applies particularly to low shots. The victim of your
uncertainty could be a stop, a picker-up, a blackberry-
picker, or someone who has innocently wandered along to
watch the sport.

Keep the gun unloaded except when you are expecting a
shot. On a rough shoot, many of the participants are often
keenly optimistic all the time and so they *always* expect or

[107]

hope for a shot and never unload! 'Got to be ready, you know. Can't tell when you might get a chance of a shot.'

With driven game, you should unload at the end of the drive. If you hear a shot after the drive is over, or when walking to the next one, you should suspect there is a dangerous Gun somewhere among the party. Never take a 'safe shot' on trust until he proves himself by his behaviour. A newcomer to a shoot went to help one of the older Guns find a bird after a pheasant drive. They poked around in some rough grass near a barbed wire fence, and presently the old Gun said, 'It may have dropped a bit farther out. I'll just have a look over the fence.' The new boy said, 'Right. Let me take your gun.' He took it, and automatically opened it as the other climbed over the wire. The gun was loaded.

All shooting men know that a gun should never be pointed at anyone, but it is still done by some – presumably without thinking. When 'coffee-housing' after a drive, you will undoubtedly see some of them with their guns closed instead of open for all the world to see that there are no cartridges in, with the muzzles pointing at other men's feet or at dogs. (Plate 43.) Waiting for a drive to begin, one of them sits on his shooting-stick with his gun horizontally across his knees, pointing at his neighbour. (Plate 44.) Another holds his gun with the trigger guard resting against the front of his shoulder, stock up and muzzles pointing at a picker-up behind him. If he turns to talk to his neighbour on one side, the gun then points at his neighbour on the other side. Farther down the line, perhaps, a young man adopts an aggressive stance – legs apart, arms vertically down, his right hand holding the grip of the gun, his left fingers under the barrels, which again point horizontally. These careless acts in holding a gun, usually loaded, are sometimes committed by experienced shots who may be old or tired or

[108]

both, and cannot be bothered to hold their guns properly. They should know that the right way is this: with the muzzles pointing at the ground, close to, or up at the sky. Safe gun-handling needs constant alertness. It can be tiring – especially when tramping over a grouse moor, for instance. But that is no excuse for carrying the gun at the trail.

Loaders can adopt some pretty perilous tactics, too. A common fault is for the loader, having received the fired gun, to turn to his left to reload, allowing the barrels – one of which may still be loaded – to swing down past the shooter's feet. Having loaded, he turns to his right – with the barrels again passing his Gun's legs before he raises them. An observant picker-up will know that this happens more often than is generally realised. The loader *should* turn to his *right* originally, lower the barrels, reload and raise the stock to close the gun, then lift the barrels towards his right front so that there is no danger of them pointing at his own Gun or at the next man along the line.

Amateur loaders can be responsible for some really fearsome exhibitions. Loading is a serious job, to be practised 'cold', using empty guns or perhaps snap caps. It is not safe to press into service as a loader an unpractised local gardener or farm worker.

One recent frantic mix-up occurred when a Gun arrived at a shoot expecting to be supplied with a loader, found none, and asked his wife to oblige. She tried but she was left-handed. No one was shot: but, equally, no one knows why!

Do not keep a loaded gun in the house. People do, and inquisitive children get shot or accidentally shoot an adult.

Look up the barrels often when out shooting, particularly in snow, or after crawling through a thick hedge or over the mud when 'fowling. Have a look quite frequently during the day: when you pick up your gun after lunch, for example, and before loading it. An earwig in the striker hole is not likely to cause much trouble, but a field mouse in the barrel will – as was discovered by a pigeon shooter who had lain down his gun in the hide.

Do not relax safety measures because you are alone. It is easy – and can be fatally so – to decide not to bother to unload when crossing an obstacle because there is no one near who might get shot, or to leave the gun loaded while you do something else. A pigeon shooter gave himself a nasty shock when he left his loaded gun leaning against the hide while he went out to fix his decoys. His dog came bumbling out of the hide and knocked the gun over. It went off. Lone shooters and those who go in for rough shooting are often a bit over-anxious not to lose the chance of a shot, but it is better to be unloaded and miss an opportunity than to be loaded and wish, too late, that you had observed the safety rules.

Other dangerous situations frequently arise when the gun has to be put down somewhere. It can be difficult. Where *do* you put the wretched thing when the ground is wet or muddy? Two principles are that the gun must be unloaded and it must be flat, not leaning against something. A gun propped against a wall might easily be knocked over by a dog (Plate 42); the barrels could be dented, and bulges would be formed by the dents when the gun is fired. Before laying down the gun, make sure that it is empty and then, if possible, put it on a car seat. If you must put it on the ground, place your hat under the action. When you pick it up, examine the barrels for dirt that may have lodged in them.

A man shot a hare and laid his gun on the ground to

[110]

pick up the animal, which was not dead. The hare kicked with its hind legs and hit the trigger of the still-loaded second barrel. As a result of the wound he sustained, the man lost his foot.

Continental shotguns are frequently fitted with a sling. It is simple to fit one to any gun, and the sling is most useful when two hands are needed to carry the 'clobber' when going out to shoot pigeon over decoys; when wildfowling, where you have to scramble in and out of muddy gutters; when rough shooting, staggering back to the car with a couple of hares, a cock pheasant and some 'various'. Another advantage in having a sling is that when you want to get rid of the gun temporarily you can hang it across your back instead of having to put it down somewhere.

Little appears in shooting literature about low birds, although the high bird is frequently discussed at length. The danger of the low bird is that the shooter, although he may be able to see that there is no one obviously standing in the line of fire, often cannot know what is beyond the bird, except in open flat country. This applies in all types of shooting.

Grouse tend to follow the curve of a hill, which means that they are often low as they pass the butts. In hilly country, the man in the uphill butt is vulnerable because a bird which appears to be fairly high to the Gun in a lower butt – and therefore shootable without obviously swinging through the line – is in reality a low bird, to be treated circumspectly. Whenever you are shooting on the side of a hill, be particularly careful about shots taken on your uphill side.

When wildfowling, low shots can be dangerous because another 'fowler may have crept up in the darkness and settled himself nearby without you knowing.

[111]

When pigeon shooting from a hide, be wary after a lull. All manner of people may have innocently wandered quite close to your position without seeing you – and if you swing round to take a low bird behind, you may hit more than you expect.

Hare shoots are notorious for rather slap-happy behaviour. No shots ought to be taken towards the beaters if they are closer than a hundred yards, preferably more. Hares should not be shot at beyond thirty yards range, although they often are, because to the inexperienced eye they look so big. There then follows the distressing sight of a wounded animal limping over the horizon. Another hazard of hare shoots is the stony nature of much downland which causes shots to ricochet, of which more will be said later. When a hare appears on a pheasant drive it should only be shot when there is plenty of open ground beyond it – not as it comes out of the covert towards the Guns, and not even behind the gunline if there is another wood there fifty yards or so away. The wood in front may well conceal a stop and the one behind a picker-up, both of whose whereabouts are unknown to the shooter. Because of the danger, many pheasant-shoot hosts issue an edict: 'No ground game.'

Greedy shooting, apart from being bad form, is also dangerous when low birds are the target. Here, again, the rough shooter in the company of friends ought to be even more careful than usual. 'A' unwittingly shot 'B' through a hedge a few years ago when they were working their dogs along it and turning out the odd pheasant or two. The blow dealt by even fairly spent shot is most surprisingly powerful, and 'B' was knocked flat. 'A' looked through the hedge, saw his friend and thought he must have killed him. But it turned out that the thick jacket 'B' was wearing had absorbed most of the pellets, although two or three had penetrated his

[112]

hands and one was lodged far enough into the flesh above his eyebrow to require hospital attention.

The manner in which shot can ricochet is sometimes very startling. Any hard surface may cause it: a tree, quite small stones, frozen ground, or the side of a building. The only way to avoid it is to ensure that there is a good area of clear sky beyond your bird – which, of course, is not always possible. On one occasion a very good and experienced shot fired at a grouse behind his butt at about 45° to the line of butts. Some pellets struck a rock and ricocheted through 90°. A few of them hit the face of a lady in the next butt. The shooter was exonerated from blame for what was regarded as a freak accident; but he felt bound to accompany the victim, who was not seriously hurt, to a doctor. This happened on the first drive and the unfortunate guest thus lost his rare opportunity of a day's grouse shooting. But he now has every reason to be aware of the unexpected effect of a ricochet.

Complete safety in the shooting field comes only with experience of all forms of shooting, on all types of ground, and at all the different sorts of quarry. Any degree of acquired safety tends to lapse when the shooter is confronted with a new situation, or when he is cold or tired or anxious. Since the rough shoot is usually a training ground for at least a few novices, it unfortunately carries an element of risk rather higher than wildfowling – when the shooter is less liable to be in range of other Guns – or the formal shoot, where the Guns are usually more experienced. The longer you shoot the more chance there is of discovering that shooting accidents do not happen only to other people. But to ensure that *you* are not going to be the cause of an accident, never take on trust the safeness of a gun, a man or a situation until you have investigated them.

[113]

CHAPTER SIX

WILDFOWLING

'OF all forms of shooting for sport there is none so natural, so varied and so fascinating as that of wildfowling.'

This is a quotation from one of the many books by the late N. M. Sedgwick, whose writings under the name of 'Tower-Bird' for so long delighted readers of the weekly paper *Shooting Times*. Its truth would never be denied by anyone who has enjoyed the sport.

The setting is always exhilarating, whether under the startling changes of a red and gold dawn sky or the black scudding clouds of a wild winter's afternoon. The tang of the restless sea, the smell of the mud and the cry of the waders, busy along the tideline, all combine to make a man's heart beat faster.

But wildfowling is not for everyone. To some it is too lonely, and too uncomfortable, and too unsatisfying when the bag is small or non-existent. To be a really successful wildfowler requires an immense amount of study and experience of the birds, and of the places they frequent. Of course, it is possible to enjoy 'fowling without a great deal of previous knowledge. But the full pleasure is lacking unless the 'fowler is happy in the wildness of his surroundings and finds the loneliness refreshing rather than distressing. True wildfowling is not a sport to pursue merely because the would-be shooter thinks that it is 'free'.

Inland duck shooting on flight ponds, or shooting geese –

either on a Scottish loch or feeding in the fields – is not wild-fowling in the accepted sense. The real sport takes place by the sea-wall and out over the mud-flats, where the gutters meander seawards and the wind and the tide control the actions of hunter and hunted. But the foreshore is not owner-less land where anybody may go and shoot.

The foreshore belongs to the Crown or to private indi-viduals. The only rights the public have over it are those of navigation and fishing. The owners of a foreshore may, and often do, lease their shore and the sporting rights over it. The landward limit of the foreshore is the average line of the high tides occurring in the mid period between ordinary springs and neaps. The marsh, saltings, merse, or whatever it may be called, which lies inland of this line, is seldom foreshore and belongs to the owner of the adjoining land. The public has no legal right to shoot over the foreshore.

The Firearms Act, 1965, made it unlawful to be in a public place with a loaded shotgun and without authority. The foreshore is a public place within the meaning of the Act. Technically, therefore, anyone shooting on Crown foreshore, other than in Scotland, is a trespasser. For this reason, the Wildfowlers Association of Great Britain and Ireland obtained an authority from the Crown Estate Com-missioners which permits members of W.A.G.B.I. to shoot on Crown foreshore. Anyone who is not a member of W.A.G.B.I., and therefore not covered by this authority, does so at his own risk. For other than Crown land, the wild-fowler must obtain permission from the owner of the fore-shore he proposes to visit.

Access to a foreshore is frequently across private land, and for permission to cross this the owner or the tenant must be approached. Even when the necessary authority to go wild-fowling has been granted, it is illegal to shoot game.

Although this may all sound depressingly negative, it is intended only to show that shore shooting is not a free-for-all in which anybody can wander around with a gun and take a shot at more or less anything. Unfortunately, however, the rights of the matter are still ignored by a few irresponsible owners of guns, the worst of whom are known as 'marsh cowboys'. Not all searchers after free shooting belong to this tribe. Many keen and honest youngsters believe that they are entitled to shoot duck by the sea – and geese, too, if they can find them. Their reasoning seems to be: 'God put them there. No one really owns them; so why shouldn't we have them?' It is much the same as the attitude of some people towards the picking of mushrooms or black-berries on privately-owned land; although the landowner for long has raised no objection, the right to do so cannot be acquired by custom.

Some of the carefree approach to wildfowling, even by those who have tried to find out something about it, may be due to reading books on the subject which are now out of date. Hemmed in as we are by restrictions, it becomes more and more difficult to keep up to date with the law on almost anything. If you read some of the wildfowling classics by Millais or Payne-Gallwey, for instance, you will find the author discussing the shooting of many birds – such as swans, barnacle geese, and various waders – which are now protected. Or you may hear of lucky salmon fishermen who have paid for their holiday by selling the fish they caught and therefore reason that a successful 'fowling trip to some Scottish firth might be partly paid for by selling the geese that are shot. But to do this now would be illegal.

We must believe that all the legislation is intended to be

in the interests of most of us in the long run – and, incidentally, that it is for the benefit of the birds we wish to shoot. As long ago as the 1880s, Payne-Gallwey was writing 'fowl are getting scarcer and gunners more numerous every year'. This is a familiar cry. Similarly, referring to the decline in the sport of fishing, Thomas Bastard gave as the reason: 'Fishes decrease, and fishers multiply.' This was in 1598!

More sportsmen pursuing less game, in the widest sense, inevitably leads to control. It has to be accepted, but it makes it more difficult for the newcomer to take up the sport. On several parts of the coast where 'free' shooting was once available, the rights have now been acquired by a local club with a limited membership. All is not lost, however, and perseverance and a request for help will nearly always produce results; although there is no doubt that wildfowling in the 1980s is beset by a good many restrictions.

A most important aspect of the sport is that of recognising the quarry. No longer is the shooter faced only with pheasants and rabbits, which everyone knows. There are many different species of birds, each having its own characteristics of habit, flight, edibility, and so on. The wild geese which regularly winter in Great Britain are greylag, whitefront, pinkfoot, and bean – all of which normally rest at night on a sandbank, or some similarly inaccessible spot in the estuary of their choice, and fly inland to feed by day in the fields. The black geese – barnacle and brent – usually feed along the coastline, and they may not be shot. Canada geese are generally only semi-wild and live on inland park lakes. They fly out to nearby fields to feed and may legally be shot – but this is not wildfowling.

Duck may be divided into either surface feeders or divers, and they have varying culinary attractions as well as

[117]

differences in being legally shootable or not (see Appendix G). The characteristic that interests the 'fowler is that many of them fly inland in the evening to feed and back out to sea around dawn to rest – the reverse of the way of geese.

Waders flit along the edge of the tide-line and probe around in the mud exposed by the tide. Their shrill calls provide incessant background noise to the hidden 'fowler waiting for the rustle of mallard pinions, the whistle of widgeon, and the thrilling hound-music of geese.

Although geese are normally day-feeders, they may feed at night under a bright moonlit sky, flighting out to sea at dawn. Duck, too, sometimes flight under the moon. Indeed, any unusual weather conditions can cause a change in what is regarded as the normal behaviour of birds. In very calm weather, duck may float about on the flat sea and refuse to fly inland – to the chagrin of the 'fowler. But when it is very rough and a high tide pushes them off the mud flats, the shore gunner hopes for extra sport during the day, apart from the expected morning and evening flights. He studies the times of the tides and the time that the moon and sun rise and set; he tries to discover where the birds are feeding; and then he works out a plan of campaign to be modified, like that of every good general, according to the circumstances of the moment.

You can stalk wildfowl among the creeks left by the receding tide and you can wait for them on their feeding or resting grounds, although this is generally to be deprecated. But the essence of the business is to intercept them on their flight lines – which calls for skill in deciding where to go, because the lines change according to weather conditions and chosen feeding areas. (Plate 45.) A dawn flight, for example, may begin with some duck coming out from the land while it is still dark: you will hear them, but you will

[118]

not see many. Then the gulls start drifting inland, and presently the curlew come too. You may shoot these and they can be made edible. The waders are busy in front of your hide and perhaps you will shoot a redshank, if you know what it looks like. But you may not shoot a green-shank. Finally, when you are just about to go back for breakfast, the geese far out in front spring into the air with a wild clamour and flight inland, but too high and wide for a shot. And then suddenly some more geese appear, flying low and straight across in front of your hide. But they are brent, and so you leave them alone. There is a useful little pamphlet issued by W.A.G.B.I. called *Know Your Quarry*. A practical way of seeing several varieties of duck and geese is to visit the Severn Wildfowl Trust at Slimbridge, which is about twelve miles south-west of Gloucester.

Only experience can teach you to recognise birds in the wild by their wing-beats or their call – especially in poor light. The novice can, for example, easily mistake a low teal for a high mallard and vice versa. Knowledge of some of the other aspects of fowling – like details of equipment needed – can, however, be acquired from books and the advice of more experienced shooters.

A standard game gun is often quite suitable, although a Magnum which can take 3-inch cartridges is better if geese are expected. The big-bore guns are somewhat outmoded now, except for the especially enthusiastic chap who may get more fun out of his gun than what he shoots with it. An 8-bore is quite a possession, and is as much a talking point as a vintage Bentley. But both are expensive to run. The shooter who can make fairly frequent trips to the coast will probably equip himself with a 3-inch Magnum in addition to his game gun, but if he can only afford the latter he will not be at very much of a disadvantage.

[119]

If you do buy yourself a wildfowling gun, remember to check it on the pattern plate and have it regulated, if necessary, with the same type of cartridge you intend to use. Many of these guns are too tightly choked to be of much use under about thirty yards range, and some of the old ones may be so worn as to throw very irregular patterns at any range. Do have a sling fitted: you will never regret it. It always seems strange that this advice, though readily agreed, is so rarely acted upon. Payne-Gallwey gave it ninety years ago in his Badminton Library book on shooting, and he once had good reason for regretting the absence of a sling. He laid down his gun while he went to look for a bird on an Irish snipe bog and a nimble native picked it up and ran off with it.

The gun will have to withstand rougher treatment than normal and a few extra precautions are advisable. Before going out, the inside and outside of the barrels should be wiped dry of oil to prevent sand sticking to them. Nowadays, the non-corrosive primers used in modern cartridges, coupled with the wiping action of the impregnated wad, have made gun-cleaning much easier. In fact, not much harm would ensue if the gun were to be put away uncleaned after a normal day's shooting – although such a habit is not advocated. Sea-water, however, is another matter altogether, and the wildfowler's gun should be carefully cleaned and dried as soon as possible after use. A feather or a pipe cleaner should be pushed into all crevices where salt-water may lurk – such as where the triggers enter the action, and behind the extractors. Some 'fowlers paint their gun-barrels grey or green as camouflage. If you try this, you ought to remove the paint at the end of the season to check for corrosion along the rib. Painting a gun is scarcely worth while and it can conceal a dangerous situation which needs putting right.

Waterproof cartridges are advisable, as are bigger shot sizes than usual: BB or No. 1 for geese and probably No. 5 for duck. It is easy to become bemused over shot sizes. If you are going to walk a marsh after snipe, it would be sensible to use No. 8. For teal, No. 7 might be best; whereas a high old mallard could require No. 4 in the choke barrel. So the fully equipped shooter takes several different cartridges on his wildfowling trip, from 2½-inch No. 8 to 3-inch BB. Unfortunately, he often has the wrong ones in his gun at any particular moment. A simple compromise is to stick to 6's all the time but to carry some 1's in a special pocket, ready to be loaded as soon as geese are heard. In a game gun, No. 1 gives a better pattern than BB, which is more suited to fairly long-range shooting with a tightly choked wildfowling gun.

Among the 'fowler's equipment should be a torch, a cartridge extractor, and a pull-through. The last, consisting of a lead weight on one end of a piece of string with a rag at the other end, can save the day if the gun is inadvertently dropped in the mud and the barrels become blocked. (Plate 47.) A piece of stick may be needed first to poke out the main blockage.

A compass can be a life-saver, for even the most experienced wildfowler sometimes loses his bearings. One who was very sure of himself, and often advised others to beware of fog and tides, decided to go out alone on the estuary one night. Conditions were good. The tide was right; there was plenty of wind; there was no chance of fog and so he walked out to where he reckoned he would be under the flight line. There was no other gunner about and he knew he could stay in position until the flowing tide just reached him. There would be only one way back, but some shore lights would guide him straight to the crossing point

[121]

over the main gutter behind him. He had not bothered to bring a compass.

The duck came over and he had some great shooting, but soon it was time to move back. He stayed for a ccuple more shots, and as he was picking up his birds some big flakes of snow began to fall. He just had time to check a line on the shore lights and then he began to walk hurriedly back. But the snow became blinding and, to his horror, he found the water was getting deeper. He had been walking in a half-circle. He tried to retrace his steps and work out where he was – he who thought he knew these mudflats like the back of his hand. Visibility was nil, and the water was up to his knees. Then he heard a train moving along the line near the shore and was able to get a rough bearing from it. Thoroughly alarmed now, he set off as fast as he could, dumping first the duck and then the cartridge bag. He was on the point of dropping his gun and preparing to swim when he suddenly came to the edge of the snowstorm and could see the line of lights some way off to his left. He struggled on, with the water up to his armpits, and just reached the shore in time. Completely soaked and very exhausted, he staggered across the fields to the road, where there was an inn. He pulled open the door and collapsed – safe, and very lucky.

The shooting of wildfowl is affected by a few minor complications, the first of which is range. It is often more difficult to judge range in the bare landscape than it is inland among trees and hedges. With experience, you can learn how visible the markings of a bird are when it is in range, and how big it then looks. Try to avoid over-long shots which result in the birds only being pricked. This sometimes happens with geese, whose large sizes makes them appear to be closer than they are. Their slow wing-beats are also

[122]

deceptive. You should watch their heads and swing out well in front, because they fly faster than you might think.

Two other difficulties are footwork in the mud and swinging a gun when wearing heavy clothing. Although you cannot move your feet quickly if they are stuck in soft ground, you can pivot from the hips for more than a right-angle to each side, as mentioned in Chapter One. The novice should practise this pivoting, swinging the gun on to gulls or waders which he is not going to shoot. When you have to crouch down in a ditch as duck approach, it is usually better to stand up to take the shot, especially in bad light. If you must shoot from a kneeling position, it is particularly helpful to have a few practice swings from the cramped position before birds appear. Convince yourself that you can pivot your body round without merely swinging your arms across it. Lean forward for the overhead shot : if you rock back on to your right heel, the swing will be checked.

It is always wise to have a special 'fowling gun fitted while you are wearing the appropriate warm clothing. If you find the stock of your normal gun is a little too long when wearing heavy clothing, you can help matters by pushing your arms and gun out in front of you just before preparing for a shot. The movement is similar to shooting a cuff. It straightens out some of the folds of clothing round your shoulders and helps gun mounting. The rubber recoil pad, that somewhat extraneous fitting, is best avoided because it is particularly liable to catch the extra clothing and prevent the butt from sliding easily into the shoulder.

A technical point about range arises from the fact that some shooters claim that their guns seem to have a less effective range over water than over land. The explanation lies firstly in the fact that it is much more difficult to estimate range over water than land, and so the shooter may be

[123]

expecting too much from his gun, and secondly in the changed ballistics of a gun fired at sea-level in a cold temperature and low barometric pressure compared with the time it was pattern tested, perhaps on a warm, high-pressure summer day, five hundred feet above sea-level, inland.

Concealment is important. Even the very slight cover provided by a post or a gate is better than being right out in the open. It is worth trying to base any duck hide on a permanent feature, like a fence; and flotsam, such as an oil drum or bits of wood, should be used. (Plate 46.) A piece of sacking daubed with brown dye or permanganate of potash is easily carried in the game bag and is useful for tying on to a fence or bush. A light portable hide, suitable for erection away from any natural feature, can be made of sacking supported on bamboo poles about 4 ft. long. The front and sides should be pegged out so that they are sloping, not vertical. Holes or gaps between the pieces of sacking will allow the wind to blow through rather than blow the whole thing over. The outline must be as low as possible – only about 3 ft. above the ground. The occupant sits in the hide with his feet in a hole and his left shoulder to the front.

An essential piece of equipment for making any hide, even in an unadorned natural gutter, is a digging implement. One of the easiest to carry is an ordinary gardening trowel. With this you can scrape out a flat shelf to sit on or dig a small hole for your feet. Hide 'furniture' should include something to sit on, like an old bit of plastic macintosh or a collapsible stool of the Tower-Bird type. (Plate 48.) The stool consists of two pieces of wood about nine inches square. On to the bottom one is fixed an electric-light pendant cover. One end of a piece of $\frac{3}{4}$-inch pipe, fourteen inches long and screw-threaded at each end, screws into this. The top piece of wood has a swivel domed pendant cover fixed on to it and the other end of the vertical pipe is then screwed into it. The pipe must be screwed into a metal holder and not directly into the wood, because in the latter case it could eventually perforate right through the wood with most uncomfortable results. The bottom plate prevents the stool from sinking into mud and the top one provides a swivel seat for the 'fowler. The pipe and connections are obtainable from ironmongers. The stool is easily carried when taken to pieces, and can be remarkably comfortable during a long wait; it is possible to shoot without getting up from a seated position.

Although one would like to dig down when making a hide, it is nearly always impracticable, even on sand, because the hole fills with water. You must build up a little, sit, and dig down only for foot space.

An original type of hide was once thought up by an enthusiastic novice who had yet to shoot a goose. There was a large marsh which the birds visited daily, but they came in very high and were unapproachable once they were down. The lad saw an imitation grass mat in a shop and conceived his plan : to lie under the mat in the middle of the marsh, jump up when the birds landed and quickly fire off half a dozen shots before they could get away. He even promised a goose to a friend, but would not let him into the secret of how it was to be obtained. The next day he had to admit that his idea turned into a fiasco.

'I got out to the marsh in good time, and had to wait an hour before I heard the geese. Then I lay under my mat and the plan worked beautifully; they came in and pitched all round me. They seemed so close I think I could have reached out and grabbed one. I was making up my mind exactly what I was going to do, when I heard a heavy thumping on the ground. I wondered what on earth it could be, and then discovered it was my own heart beating! I tried to keep very calm. . . . Two cartridges between the fingers of my left hand, some more ready on the ground and the gun loaded. I took off the safety catch; a bit risky but it was the chance of a lifetime. I drew a deep breath, and jumped up. . . . There was a terrific clamour, quite frightening, and the air seemed full of flapping wings. But I couldn't push the damned safety catch forward. By the time I had looked down and seen that it was already off I was getting frantic. I banged off a couple of hurried shots, and then I dropped the spare cartridges I had ready. By then the geese were a hundred yards away and I was swearing words I didn't even know I knew!'

Fowl can be attracted by calling them or by decoys. Calling is an art that is best learnt by instruction on the spot – which means that you have to find an expert and persuade him to teach you. This, unfortunately, is not at all easy. It is not too difficult, however, for the untrained to call small parties of geese that are not quite sure where they are going; and a lone goose is even easier. If you just open your mouth wide and shout a sort of *aah-unk* noise, there is a good chance of turning the birds towards you. But it is a complete waste of effort to try to call a big skein of geese flighting inland to a known feeding area which they have already chosen.

Various wind instruments are on the market which, when blown, are supposed to sound like ducks or geese. They nevertheless require a certain skill to be effective. One of the better ones, for mallard, is a concertina-shaped rubber tube which, when shaken, emits the kind of burbling noise ducks make when they are feeding. Some 'fowlers make a whistle, to imitate wigeon, out of the brass ends of two cartridge cases which they fix together after removing the primers. It is important when calling to distinguish between the varying notes used by a bird in differing circumstances. You are unlikely to attract a bird by using its alarm call – as, for instance, the well known *kurr-lee* of the curlew.

Some waders may be called by arousing their curiosity. Curlew, for example, will sometimes fly over to mob a piece of brown paper waved by the hidden gunner. Or instead of waving his bit of paper, the shooter can tie it to a piece of string secured by a stone and let it blow about in the wind.

Decoys in the shape of ducks or geese can be made from wood, papier mâché or rubber. Even simple silhouettes, with no bulk, are effective when the birds' approach line can be fairly acurately estimated. The home-manufacture of decoys is dealt with in Michael Shephard's book (Appendix J) and *The Complete Wildfowler*, written by Duncan and Thorne about seventy years ago. Of the ready-made ones, self-inflating rubber decoys are the easiest to carry : they take up so little room in the game bag. (Plates 49, 50.) But in fact, decoys are seldom of much use off the coastline. It is difficult to display them properly in flowing water and they do not seem to have much attraction. But on a pool in the marsh, or a 'splash', or a flooded meadow, they can be a great draw.

When flighting, one often has to shoot in the dark – which emphasises the need for a properly fitted gun. Devices like putting a blob of mud or chewing gum on the end of the barrels in order to see where the gun is pointing represent wrong thinking. When you mount your gun properly, it points where you are looking. Often, you will hear but not see approaching duck, and so you will not be able to put the muzzles on the line of a bird in preparation for the shot. You will have to look up with the gun half mounted; and directly you see the dark shape nearly overhead, you must shoot as quickly as possible, relying on the gun following your eye.

This is the one exception to the rule of putting the muzzles on the line before mounting the gun.

Retrieving shot birds is often difficult without a dog, and the rule is always to go out and collect them as soon as possible. There may be safety reasons for not taking a dog, but if you are going to have one with you, take along something for it to sit on during a long wait. A piece of sacking will suffice. The dog will often look colder than it is. As long as it has not been treated too softly at home, and been allowed to spend most of its time sleeping by the fire, its natural coat will have grown sufficiently thick to protect it. Proper gundogs are remarkably hardy. It is a bit unfair, though, to expect a pampered pet to sit out in a blizzard without any previous toughening-up period.

Recipes for cooking most shootable fowl exist, but rarely in the recognised cook-books. Indeed, those books that mention the cooking of game usually advise too short a time in the oven. A longer time at a lower heat is preferable, although some people prefer mallard – called 'wild duck' in the books – to be underdone. When you do find a recipe, the sauce is apt to be the most important feature: and it must be admitted that the unadorned muddy or fishy taste of some sea-feeding duck is not to everyone's fancy. You should skin a curlew; and you might try putting an onion in the crop of a shore-feeding duck late in the season. A stubble-feeding mallard in September makes excellent eating with any doctoring.

The essential point is to hang all game, including wildfowl, for a reasonable time: three or four days in a warm September, three weeks or more in a freezing January. Hanging does not make the meat bad; it makes it tender and gives it a better flavour. In the days before deep-frozen

High Tide

51. They are crossing a ditch by a plank permanently fixed in place. A slightly higher tide will cover the plank, but the post on the right is a guide. The danger of being cut off by the tide is particularly serious in fog or snow.

Low Tide

52. This sort of gutter may be crossed easily at low water on the way out to the tideline, but it will be impassable at high tide.

A BOAT IN THE REEDS

53. A small rowing boat, hidden in the reeds, makes a wildfowler's hide. One teal has been shot; the labrador looks bored as she waits for some more work.

THE GAME CART

54. A labrador guards a useful bag of partridges, pheasants, hares and a few pigeon. A young dog should not be left with game in a car until it can be trusted not to eat it.

Low Partridges

55. As they skim over the hedge they are too close to shoot in front. He follows them with his left hand, keeping the muzzles up, and will take the shot behind him, to the right.

56. A covey of partridges over the guns. They are high enough for two guns to fire at them at once.

A Flapping Decoy

58. The body is wood and the detachable wings are made of talc. A string to operate the wings leads down from them through an eye at the bottom of the stick and out to the shooter in his hide; it should be darker than the light string used to show up in the photograph.

Decoys from Gumboots

57. The boot has been marked out ready for cutting. F is the part which makes the "feeder"; S makes the "sitter" and W is the wasted part. The completed decoys are shown in front.

A PIGEON HIDE

59. Wooden supports, wire-netting and sacking. The front of the hide is camou-
flaged with pieces of straw.

A NATURAL PIGEON DECOY

A useful addition to dead
ds lying on ground with heads
opped up is one impaled on a
ippy stick, with wings held out
eways by thin string tied to
other sticks.

AN ACROSS-EYED STOCK
61. Shotgun with an across-eyed
stock. The best solution if the
shooter has a very strong left
master-eye.

GROUSE

62. Grouse, coming at you! They swerve and jink and their aerobatics and wildness ma[ke]
them one of the most difficult shots.

PICKERS-UP

63. Working partners. The pickers-up add a great deal to the bag.

beef and broiler chickens all meat was hung. The old-fashioned chicken hanging in the poulterer's shop, complete with feathers and 'innards', had a bit of flavour for that reason. Its modern counterpart which is killed, plucked, drawn and stuffed into a plastic bag almost in one motion can never taste as good.

Birds are normally hung by the neck; but in warm weather at the beginning of the season it may be better to hang them by the feet, with the wings hanging open to allow air to circulate round the body. A squirt with an aerosol fly-spray is a sensible precaution, particularly round the beak and vent. You can remove some of the nastier insides with a piece of wire bent into a small hook at the end, like a bicycle-wheel spoke: insert it per rectum, twist, and withdraw. When you draw a bird properly, be careful not to damage the gall bladder. It has a horrible flavour. If it has been damaged by shot, wash the inside of the bird particularly thoroughly.

There is an old Norfolk dish called oystercock pie which consists of one or two dozen oysters in a bucket, to which is added more or less anything that has been shot: redshank and snipe; teal and mallard; and, if the bucket is not filled, a hare! One famous meal was reputedly created from a swan stuffed with a goose stuffed with a pheasant stuffed with a wigeon stuffed with a teal stuffed with a woodcock stuffed with a snipe. When cooked, the dish was opened up and its inventor ate the snipe.

A more practicable and very delicious game recipe is pheasant stuffed with woodcock. The art lies in boning the birds. This can be done by slitting them up the back and working round to the breast, cutting off the outer wing joints, which are too finicky. The pheasant is then laid breast downwards with the woodcock on top of it. A piece of pâté should go on next, and the whole thing is then folded up, tied and skewered, and roasted. Variations of which bird is stuffed with what can be tried as long as the cook's patience lasts. The wildfowler should remember that there is a way of cooking anything he may legally shoot, and there is little point in shooting a bird if he is not prepared to eat it.

Clothing for wildfowling must be suitable for the job, which means that the outer garments should be drab-coloured – probably dark green – and windproof. It is better to wear several thin garments, such as a string vest, shirt and cashmere jersey, rather than a thick bulky sweater beneath the top-coat. Old-fashioned long pants are sensible and can still be bought at Marks & Spencer's. A wide-brimmed deerstalker-type hat and long thigh boots, not gumboots, are essential.

It is false economy to make do with any old clothes. You cannot shoot if you do not keep warm, and it is common sense to take adequate precaution against being soaked and frozen stiff. Several of the shooting coats available are not cheap. For normal use inland, a good tweed jacket is fine – especially when made with a pleat in the back and pivot sleeves. Loden cloth is becoming popular, and it is warm and water-repellent. Wool whipcord is very hard-wearing. These coats, in 1980, cost from £30–£60. For wildfowling, the coat should be long enough to keep rain from dripping into one's boots and it should be waterproof. 'Maxproof' is a trade name for a very good material for such coats; it is made of a waxed cotton, originally made by Barbour, of South Shields, who offer a range of coats, lightweight and easily folded for carrying, or heavyweight with warm liners. This material, incidentally, only retains its waterproof qualities if periodically treated with a special dressing. A good, cheap, really waterproof coat is the Bradsport Mountain coat from Hebden Cord, of Hebden Bridge, at about £20. If you buy some sort of anorak jacket with a hood, you can ignore the hood. It may keep the draught off the back of your neck, but the rustling in your ears as you turn your head will prevent you from hearing the fowl.

Three of the very best items for shooting wear – waistcoat, socks, and jacket – come from Husky of Tostock, who make quilted nylon clothing at Stowmarket, in Suffolk. Quilted nylon is extremely light and warm, but it does not make the wearer insufferably hot when he is hurrying along to reach his place in time for morning flight. The waistcoat is warmer and far less bulky than any sweater; the socks are excellent in thigh boots, particularly when there is snow on the ground; the jacket really does allow freedom to the shoulders, and it does not tear on thorns or barbed wire. This jacket bears the rather strange name 'The Executive', but it is none the less suitable for the labourer or the lord. It may look a bit smart for 'fowling, although it is a sensible shade of dark green, but it is one of the best all-purpose coats. It is easily washable and it does not sweat inside, as many of the non-porous ones do. Cost in 1980, about £40.

Keeping the hands warm is difficult. Tough farmers can walk about the Wash on a December evening wearing no gloves at all. Lesser mortals feel the cold. Even the hardiest man is sometimes so numbed that his trigger finger just will not operate. Mittens are good, if they are long enough to cover the wrist. Leather gloves, perhaps silk-lined, are better; but they should have the trigger finger, or at least the top joint of it, exposed. If you use ordinary leather gloves, cut the index finger of the right-hand one half through at the first joint. This allows the top inch or so of the glove to be folded back off the finger, where it can be retained by a press stud, the two parts of which are sewn on to the top of the end of the glove-finger and on to the top of its middle joint respectively. The end of your finger can then remain bare to feel for the trigger; and you can undo the stud and push the glove back on again to keep the finger warm when you are not expecting a shot.

Having decided what sort of warm gloves you prefer, the next problem is how to keep them dry. One way is to buy a pair of thin gauntlets, such as motor cycle shops sell, made of 'Maxproof' or P.V.C. – but not great thick leather ones. They will fit on easily and prevent the warming gloves from being soaked as you scrabble your way out across muddy gutters or under other such non-shooting conditions. When you are expecting a shot and if it is raining or snowing, connect the thumb of your right-hand gauntlet to your waist with a piece of string, and push your hand only half-way into the gauntlet. When you want to shoot, merely pull your right hand out and the secured gauntlet will fall away, leaving you with a warm gloved hand with a bared index finger ready to operate. Those who use them claim remarkable success for pocket hand-warmers, which operate on solid fuel.

A final piece of clothing is a pair of shorts, preferably waterproof, to be worn over normal trousers. It is possible to buy some made of 'Maxproof', but an old pair of golfing trousers can be cut down for the purpose. They are not expected to keep your bottom dry if you sit in a puddle, but they will keep the mud off your behind when you kneel. This can be a considerable comfort in a very muddy estuary like The Wash.

Almost classified as clothing because they should always be worn are binoculars. The large ones favoured by race-goers are unnecessarily powerful and heavy. A small monocular is quite adequate, and it fits easily into a breast pocket. It is needed for identifying birds, particularly when they are on the ground. And it is also useful for identifying people – when, for instance, you see another 'fowler in the distance and wonder whether he is a friend or an encroacher on 'your' bit of foreshore.

The dangers of wildfowling have often been described but even more often ignored, usually by keen but ignorant youngsters. Unfortunately, some people can be persuaded of the potential danger of uncertain situations only after they have been involved in difficulties and escaped. Many dangers can be reduced if you get to know your particular piece of shoreline under all conditions. A new area should be treated with respect and caution. The trouble is that 'fowlers are inclined to lose their discretion in the excitement of shooting.

Mud and quicksand can be deathtraps, but usually only when the victim walks in carelessly and then panics. If you find yourself really sinking in soft ground, you should throw yourself backwards at once and try to roll out, even if you are in a few inches of water. This will be effective if done in time. Otherwise, all you can do is lean out with your arms spread flat on the ground, the gun held between them, and shout for help.

A keen pheasant and partridge shooter suddenly 'discovered' wildfowling. At least, he heard stories about it, and asked a local 'fowler to take him out. Eventually, this worthy reluctantly agreed, telling the gentleman not to wear his best shooting suit, and not to bring his spaniel because they would be going on to some difficult mudflats. Needless to say, the novice arrived smartly dressed and with his dog.

After a short way over the mud he said, 'By Jove, this

stuff is a bit sticky, isn't it? The poor dog is up to its belly. I thought he might retrieve my birds but perhaps I shall have to retrieve him!'

They plodded on and the 'fowler placed his gentleman ready for the evening flight, and went on a further couple of hundred yards himself. They had a few shots and just as it became dark there were shouts for help. The guest was stuck in the mud and could not move. He had tried to prize himself out with his gun and it was muzzles down with the butt barely showing; the dog was bogged too, and whimpering sadly. The tide was coming in.

'Do exactly as I say', ordered the 'fowler. 'Keep calm, or you'll have me in too.'

With the help of his belt he gradually managed to pull the victim out a little, and then told him to lie on his back and try to wriggle his legs out of his boots, one at a time. This was successful.

'Now keep still, while I look for the gun.'

'Oh, leave it. Don't bother. I'm too cold.'

The gun was recovered, and found to be still loaded. The 'fowler took out the cartridges.

'Now I'll try to help the dog', he said.

'No, don't. Just shoot him and leave him. I must get out of here.' The voice rose, a trifle shrill; panic wasn't far away.

The 'fowler released the dog and led the way back to the car, where they all piled in, mud and all. The tension relaxed, but their troubles were not yet over.

When they reached the gentleman's house his wife met them at the door. 'Hullo, darling', he said, cheerfully. 'Sorry we're a bit late. Could you get us a couple of large whiskies, please?'

'Whiskies be damned!' was the reply. 'You don't come

[134]

in here like that. You can wash in a bucket of water by the garage. I'll throw out some clothes for you. And get rid of that horrible stray dog behind there. What have you done with ours? Lost him, I suppose. To hell with your wild-fowling!' The door slammed.

Fog as a danger should be sufficiently obvious, but it is frequently ignored until too late. The trouble is that it causes the birds to fly lower than usual and sometimes to circle around while they try to get their bearings: and so the 'fowler stays to make the most of the shooting and then finds that he, too, has lost his bearings. Snow can be even more dangerous because of the suddenness of its oncoming. At the appearance of either fog or snow, the shooter should immediately retreat until he is safe from the tide.

Unusual accidents can happen to the lone wildfowler, but they have to be accepted in the same way as those which may befall the lone sailor or mountain climber. It is safer, of course, for 'fowlers to go out in pairs, at least, in order that one may help another or call out a search party if something goes wrong. This is evidenced by the experience of two friends who were out on the saltings one frosty December night. One of them was shooting from a sunken tub. There were several duck moving in the bright moonlight, but it was almost windless and they were very high. Because the birds were out of shot to the other man, who had only a game gun, he decided to give up before the pre-arranged time and walked across towards his friend, who was using a Magnum gun. As he drew near, he called to his pal, who replied: 'I shall have to get out of here soon. Tide's coming up. Just going to wait a little longer. You can do the re-trieving for me!'

Presently, two mallard came over very high. The man in

the tub took the first one and killed it, and then fired at the second bird. His watching friend heard a commotion by the tub and 'a large splash, then silence. He hastened forward. The first mallard had fallen straight on to the shooter's face as he fired at the second. It had broken his nose and knocked him unconscious, and he had fallen out of the tub into the surrounding water. By the fortunate chance of his friend being near, he was quickly picked up and revived. Later, the offending duck was also retrieved – from inside the tub !

Every year there are newspaper reports of wildfowlers cut off by the tide. Nearly always, the reason for the disaster is ignorance. But acquiring the necessary knowledge is not as simple and straightforward as one might think.

In his amusing book *The Gun-punt Adventure*, Colin Willock tells how he and his 'fowling companions intentionally stood out a high tide and enjoyed a memorable duck flight. They knew their marsh and were in no danger, but a telling phrase in the description of the water being half-way up someone's waders runs: '. . . still the tide went on rising, even though the time given on the tables for full flood was now past.' Later, they discovered that the tide had been several feet higher than normal.

Although one cannot calculate precisely the time of high water, any wildfowler who goes beyond the sea-wall ought at least to try to discover what the tide is likely to do. Yet many visitors to a strange coast make little or no attempt to study the behaviour of the tide, with results often frustrating and time-wasting – and sometimes tragic. Many, apparently, have only the haziest idea of how to find out the time of high water.

Lucky 'fowlers who live near a constantly-visited coastline learn, over the years, what to expect of the sea; and they use a local tide-table as well. But those who live inland and travel considerable distances in search of geese and duck would do well to plan the dates of their weekends or shooting holidays with a knowledge of the tide conditions to be expected. How tiresome to motor a couple of hundred miles for a weekend by an estuary where the tide is dead low at noon, and during most of the short winter day the duck and waders are a mile away across impassable mudflats. A postponement of the trip for a week would assure high water at midday, with a good chance of birds along the tideline being within range.

How, then, do you find out the time of high tide in Foulmud Estuary on, say, Saturday, December 9th? 'Get a tide-table,' you say. But the chances are that when you write in October to a firm of nautical publishers for a regional almanac they will send you next year's edition, saying that this year's was sold out months ago. Well, at least you have next year's copy and can plan ahead as that season approaches. In the meantime, other sources of tidal information are *Whitaker's Almanac*, the *Automobile Association's Members Handbook* and the *Nautical Almanac* published by H.M.S.O. These are usually available in public libraries.

Perhaps some explanation of tides would be helpful, especially to those who have a vague idea that spring tides occur only in the spring of the year. Tides are caused by the attraction of the moon and, to a much smaller extent, the sun on the waters on earth. When earth, moon and sun are in line (at new moon and full moon), the gravitational pull is strongest and the highest, spring tides result. When sun and moon are at right-angles (first and third quarters of the moon's phases), we have the smaller, neap tides with a much reduced rise and fall. The actual tidal flow is modified by the shape of coastlines and the moon's motion, which

[137]

changes from north to south of the equator. Theoretical one-hundred-per-cent-accurate prediction of tides is not possible. Tables are based on past observations of times and heights. Springs and neaps do not necessarily occur at exactly the appropriate moon phase. At London Bridge, for example, spring tide is one or two days after new or full moon and neap tide is about a day after first and last quarter. The shape and depth of an estuary also affects the tides, so that we have double tides in the Solent (a complication for sailors), almost no tidal rise and fall in the Mediterranean, and one of forty feet in the Severn estuary.

Returning to our problem of discovering the times of the tide at Foulmud, while it is possible that the local paper might print high water times it is most unlikely that the landlord of the local hotel will have any but the vaguest idea of them. However, from an almanac we can find out tidal predictions for a large port not too far away and apply the Tidal Constant (T.C.) to the time given. Thus, the *Liverpool Almanac*, published by James Munro and Co. of Glasgow, gives T.C.s for places as far apart as Silloth on the Solway and Morecambe, Llandudno and Aberdovy. The T.C. is a time in hours and minutes which, when applied to the times of high water at Liverpool, will give the *approximate* time for high water at the other places listed. Suppose our Foulmud village is near a port at the head of the main estuary which is listed in the almanac as having a T.C of 'Add 1h. 10m.' We can work out times of high water at that port, 'P', as follows, remembering to correct Greenwich Mean Time in the almanac to British Standard Time when necessary.

The column 'Height at Liverpool' tells *how* high the tide is each day. Some innocent saltings-wanderers may not realise that this does vary. To summer bathers, 'high tide'

Example of Tidal Predictions—NOT factual

Date	High water, Liverpool Morn. Aft.		Tidal Constant	H.W. at 'P' Morn. Aft.		Height at Liverpool ft.	H.W. at Foulmud Morn. Aft.	
Dec. 7	01.15	13.33	+1h. 10m.	02.25	14.43	27.6		
,, 8	01.43	14.01		02.53	15.11	26.9		
,, 9	02.14	14.34		03.24	15.44	25.9		
,, 10	02.54	15.18		04.04	16.28	24.7		
,, 11	03.47	16.18		04.57	17.28	23.3		

and 'low tide' are just terms describing conditions favourable or otherwise for swimming or shrimping; but to a 'fowler, dependent on being able to cross tide-filled creeks, the height of the tide is important. The table above shows the height decreasing daily, the moon's last quarter being on December 12th. In fact, the lowest neap tide comes two days later. A point to note here is that while a neap tide is the lowest high tide it is also the highest low tide, which is important when considering 'Can I cross such-and-such a gutter even at low tide?'

Conversely, if our chosen dates coincided with a period between, say, first quarter and full moon, the height of the tide would be increasing each day. Therefore, it would be no good thinking: 'I crossed that gutter – just – at high tide today, so I can do it again tomorrow.' Tomorrow, the tide will be a foot higher; the next day, another eighteen inches higher; and so on, until the moon wanes. (Plate 51.)

The column 'High water at Foulmud' in the table can only be filled in with the help of local knowledge or by inspired guessing, depending on the distance of Foulmud from 'P' and the nature of the estuary. For instance, on a visit to the Solway you may arrive at some fairly accurate figures for high water at Dumfries – perhaps even see them in the local paper – but for times at the Nature Reserve

[139]

opposite Blackshaw Bank, some eight miles down river, a correction of perhaps 'subtract 30 minutes' would be needed.

When you have gone out over the mud and saltings at low tide and crossed some deep gutters on the way, it is not at all easy to judge the moment to return in order to cross those gutters before the flowing tide makes them impassable other than by swimming. (Plate 52.) The most expert and experienced 'fowlers make mistakes. The very least you should do is know the predicted times for high water and push a stick or some such into the ground where you can watch the water rising up it. Remember that wind behind a rising tide will push it up faster and higher, and that the speed with which flat sands can be covered may be truly terrifying – especially as the sudden change from land to water obliterates small jumpable runnels, into which it is all too easy to fall. From the predictions table above, you can see that high tide at Foulmud on the 9th should be around 3.30 p.m., shortly before dark, so that at least there is daylight for any scramble back to safety as the tide flows. A week later, with high water at about 9 p.m., you would be faced with the problem of negotiating that deep gutter in front of the sea-wall in the dark. This could be dangerous for the inexperienced and might be an influence in the choice of dates for a shooting weekend. The later high tide could also delay evening flight until the incoming duck are practically invisible in the dark, whereas high tide in the late afternoon could be propitious for a reasonably early flight.

It is a curious fact that one can sometimes hear the tide turn – and this, coupled with the evidence of one's eyes, can be useful in amending the predicted times for a particular tide. If you reckon low water is at 2 p.m. but you note the tide turning at 1.30 p.m., you will appreciate that high water is going to be half an hour earlier than you expected.

Wildfowling is controlled by many factors: fog, moonlight, direction and strength of wind, and time and height of the tide. No man can predict precisely what the tide will do, and it is often not easy to discover what it *might* do – but it is asking for trouble not to try to anticipate the tide's behaviour. It should be considered when planning a 'fowling trip and constantly borne in mind when beyond the sea-wall. Neglect the tide at your peril.

Punting has been called the cream of wildfowl shooting. Judged by the writings of those who have done it, this must be so; but today it is an esoteric branch of the sport. There are very few punts left and when, occasionally, a new one is built it is no easy matter to find a suitable big gun for it. Attempts have been made to make punt-gunning illegal, but so far – through the efforts of W.A.G.B.I. – these have been foiled. The Wild Birds Protection Acts, however, impose a limitation on the bore of a punt-gun to $1\frac{3}{4}$ inches. All that need be said here is that punting is not simply the easy slaughtering of masses of sitting birds. It is an arduous, cold, uncertain business and it is often dangerous. The punter spends hours afloat, much of the time with his wrists immersed in the water as he paddles along. When his boat is partially swamped, he may be lying in water. He may try for days or even weeks without securing a decent shot. And when his chance comes, aligning the gun and choosing the right moment to fire requires great skill. No branch of shotgun shooting makes greater demands on the man behind the gun. Incidentally, in considering shooting afloat, boats are sometimes used to go out to islands or to hide among reeds in wait for duck. (Plate 53.) But the law forbids the use of 'any mechanically-propelled boat in immediate pursuit of a wild bird' for the purpose of killing it.

The shore-gunner, too, has to work for his shooting. And

his rewards can never be measured solely by the number of birds he brings home. He must be a dull fellow who does not thrill to the wild beauty of his surroundings and respond to the challenge of his sport.

As a final item, the shooting diary or game book is especially useful in recording wildfowling days – far less as a note of what was shot than of what was seen, and of the conditions of weather, tide, moon, wind and so on. If it is written soon after the events, it will provide accurate and useful references for future visits to the same place. It will never be a waste of time.

CHAPTER SEVEN

SYNDICATES AND CLUBS

FOR the majority of shooters – those who do not possess their own land – an urgent problem is where to obtain some shooting. It will soon become apparent that they cannot hope to receive unless they are prepared to give. The giving may be a straightforward payment or it may take the form of a service, which could be either physical work or the skill of being a good and safe shot who is welcome for his contribution to the bag.

Even the youngster who cannot afford to pay much for his sport and has yet to have the opportunity of developing into a good shot will be given a chance if he perseveres. One way of starting is to help an established shoot, and the first step in this direction is to apply to the keeper. The novice will have to prove himself reliable and willing to help. He can act as a beater, and possibly do some picking-up if he has a good dog. If he is sufficiently smart, mentally and in appearance, he could learn to be a loader. There are jobs on the shoot all the year round with which the keeper may be glad of some help. If he can earn the confidence of the keeper, or whoever is in charge of the shoot, the beginner will probably be given a few privileges – maybe flighting pigeon in March and shooting them over decoys at harvest time, joining hare shoots and vermin drives and, perhaps, an end of season 'cocks only' day. Most shoots have at least

[143]

one day when tenant farmers and other friends of the shoot are asked to bring their guns.

The man who has recently acquired his first gun sometimes feels aggrieved if he cannot find anywhere to use it, even for pigeon shooting. But if he puts himself in the position of the landowner, he should realise how that person may be justifiably distrustful of allowing a stranger on his land. Many farmers are remarkably trusting, but it is up to the would-be shooter to demonstrate his worthiness and to honour the trust.

An inexpensive way to obtain permission for some sort of shooting is to join a gun club. Some clubs are primarily for wildfowling, or rough shooting, or clay pigeon, or any combination of these. The subscription varies according to the facilities the club offers, but it is unlikely to be more than a few pounds a year. The main advantage of being a member is that the club is a responsible body which enjoys the cooperation of local landowners, farmers, keepers, the Hunt and the police. Unfortunately, most clubs have a limited membership; but names can still be put on the waiting list. Election is not automatic. The club will have rules regarding suitability of candidates, and it will probably also insist on a probationary period during which new applicants will be observed, particularly to see if they are safe.

The national organisations – the British Field Sports Society, and the Wildfowlers Association of Great Britain and Ireland – exist to look after the interests of everyone who enjoys field sports. All shooting men ought to belong to at least one of these clubs, and preferably both of them. They may help to defeat a Parliamentary bill aimed at prohibiting shooting but they cannot be expected to provide shooting facilities for individuals. They will, however, give advice about shooting and addresses of gun clubs. They also issue several most informative pamphlets on all aspects of shooting.

Virtually no free shooting by right exists. More or less free shooting by custom can be obtained on some parts of the foreshore, subject to the conditions mentioned in Chapter Six. Free shooting inland by courtesy of a landowner or tenant will almost certainly be limited to pigeon, rabbits and predators. Game shooting must be paid for, and the obvious way of finding some is to join a syndicate.

A syndicate might consist of no more than three or four friends who share the modest rent and the work on a rough shoot; or it could equally well comprise eight or ten Guns who pay a big subscription and do no work at all on the shoot. Sometimes the landowner will retain a Gun and run the syndicate; but if the shooting rights are simply let to the syndicate, it is essential that one member is appointed as leader – although the opinions of the members will naturally be taken into account when decisions are made. The leader's work continues throughout the year, but it is often a good plan to allow different members to take turns at running the shooting days. Again, someone must really be in charge, making a plan beforehand and organising the day so that it runs smoothly.

There are as many problems for those who wish to join a syndicate as there are for syndicate leaders who want to make up their numbers. The price of a Gun can vary from £250–£4000, and one may reasonably expect to get what one pays for. A certain amount of investigation is therefore wise. This means visiting the ground and talking to the keeper before the shooting season, seeing what rearing is going on and noting the presence, or absence, of vermin.

Without prior investigation, a man who had recently started shooting took a Gun in a syndicate in the south of

England at £500 for ten days. He had a course of six lessons at a school and was rated by his instructor as being an above-average shot. During the whole of the following season, however, he killed only five pheasants. He discovered, too late, that the keeper was old and idle and that the land-owner's interest in the shoot was limited to the money he could make by letting out Guns.

The owner of another nearby shoot was keen to keep it going but could not afford to do so unless he ran it as a syndicate. He had one good keeper, for whom he bought eight hundred day-old pheasant chicks, and there was a small stock of wild birds. The price of a Gun was £500 for eight days. Unlike the man who was caught, one Gun in this syndicate was quite satisfied with a personal score of one hundred and sixty-one birds during the season.

The fact is that many people who join a syndicate by answering an advertisement are not able to find out much about it before the shooting starts. But the very least they should do is to take the first opportunity of seeing the Game Book and talking to other members.

The syndicate leader who is looking for new members normally hopes for a good deal more than just their money. He would like prospective members to be reasonable shots and to be safe; but it is almost impossible for him to find out about these points during an interview. Apart from a cheerful companion, the syndicate also looks for a man who will be interested in the shoot and not merely in his own performance with a gun. The selfish outlook of a minority of shooting men is sad but very difficult to alter. At the end of a drive, they wander off to talk to another Gun and then go and sit in the Land-Rover, waiting to be taken to the next stand. They leave their shot birds for the game-cart man to collect, and they do not bother to tell a picker-up about any runners or birds which have fallen into thick cover. Their lack of co-operation is their loss, too, in that they miss the interest of the many tasks demanded by the shoot.

The interviewing syndicate leader may be able to find out something about an applicant by talking to him on shooting subjects. And he will have cause to believe that a man who has not heard of $6\frac{1}{2}$-size shot, who does not know that some double-barrelled guns have single triggers, and who thinks pheasant bags are counted by the brace may be ignorant in many other matters. The applicant might not know that pickers-up stand behind the line of Guns, or that it is correct drill to unload after a drive. He might not be able to distinguish between a young September pheasant and an adult partridge; and he might think that birds of prey should be shot.

A readily-welcomed newcomer need not be a brilliant shot, but he could make up for it in other ways: by arriving punctually, bringing a disciplined dog, being good company, getting on well with the keepers and beaters, being safe at all times, and observing the rules of etiquette and the requirements of the law. He should know a modicum of natural history, tip the keeper adequately, and take an interest in the shoot throughout the year. He might well have other virtues, too – and such a man is not rare. You will find examples at all good shoots, although you will also meet others who fall short of several of these simple requirements. Perhaps one should add that the popular recruit also pays his subscription promptly.

A beginner can be unaware of the fallibility of the printed word; he should especially beware of believing anything he reads on shooting in the non-sporting press. A description of a shoot, the behaviour of birds, the costs of shooting, or the bloodthirsty nature of those who participate are frequently grossly distorted by normally responsible journalists who neither understand their subject nor bother to find out about it.

Entirely misleading accounts have appeared concerning the work of a gamekeeper, or the expenditure on cartridges by an average shooter over a season. Some of the stranger reports have mentioned 'programmed drives of sluggish, force-fed pheasants over the muzzles of stockbrokers' guns'; and, writing of pigeon shoots, 'flocks of farmers potted away all day . . . in order to frighten the birds and keep them aloft so that eventually they would all roost in one place for mass execution at dawn. Pigeons have to eat six times a day and if they are kept in the air they soon die of exhaustion.' Some honest people might believe such nonsense.

The fanfare in the newspapers each 12th August is well known, with descriptions of 'tweedy gentry popping off their rifles at little brown grouse', but some of them go further than simply having a dig at the rich. They are most misleading when they try to be informative : the keeper on a grouse moor in Spring supposedly 'inspects the eggs every day, putting a little pen over each covey at night to protect them from foxes' – a clever chap, on a 5000-acre moor ! 'Grouse feed on worms, slugs, snails and juniper berries' – no mention of the staple diet of heather. 'Cock grouse, like cock pheasant, is considered more delicious than the hen, except when the hen pheasant is with egg' – remarkable ignorance of close seasons.

It is advisable to take with a pinch of salt most shooting articles in non-sporting papers; they have experts who write on football and cricket and horse racing but rarely anyone who knows much about field sports. As a result, one reads 'funny' articles in which the jocular writer chats glibly about

[148]

shooting game on a Sunday, for instance, and some youngster may think this is all fair and above-board because he 'saw it in the papers'.

He should not, however, believe any of the following outrageous statements, all culled from various newspapers :

a) Grouse are hand-reared, and often shot in Suffolk.
b) Only the wealthiest people can afford to eat pigeon, blackcock and bustards.
c) Partridges are shot in August.
d) When pigeon shooting, you'll kill with practically every shot.
e) Geese return to their nests each evening.
f) Partridge chicks are eaten by cuckoos.

The increasing cost of shooting is partly due to the rising value of land. An idea of some of the expenses involved helps to explain the high price of a Gun in a syndicate and why many landowners can no longer afford to run their shoots privately. Costs vary considerably according to how favourable the ground is in supporting wild birds, the amount of work the syndicate members can contribute, and the access the shoot has to cheap game food. A farmers' syndicate able to obtain feed corn 'for nothing', and rearing a few birds with a part-time keeper on ground with plenty of cover, should be able to cut costs considerably. A wealthy syndicate with a big rearing programme and indifferent ground for holding wild birds has high costs – especially if the members live many miles away and cannot contribute actively towards running the shoot.

A few general figures help to explain what is involved. Shooting rents in 1980 were at a minimum of about £2 an acre. For a good established pheasant shoot they went up to as much as £4 an acre. If a shoot produces one pheasant in the bag per acre it is doing well. On an average shoot, the number of reared birds shot in the season of their release does not exceed thirty per cent. Rearing methods vary, but many shoots have found that buying day-old chicks costs very little more than buying eggs. Brooder-rearing up to six weeks old costs about £1 a bird. The price of poults from the game farm is from about £1.70–£2.20 each, according to age and sex.

A gamekeeper's wages are not less than £70 a week. With the rent of his cottage and the usual 'perks' of a suit of clothes and supplies of coal and dog food, his cost to the shoot is around £4000. Beaters cost about £7 a day each; rates have to be paid; and there will be a Land-Rover to run. Rearing equipment must be bought, maintained and shown in the accounts as its capital value depreciates. The feed bill will cover the rearing period and throughout the winter. In covert, the cost may be about 45p per bird per week. If special game strips are sown, they will cost about £100 an acre. Income is limited to the sale of game, averaging about £3 a brace.

Costs, in round figures, to a landowner who is not paying rent or rates might work out like this:

Gamekeeper	£4000
Land-Rover	1000
Beaters	1600
Food	3000
3000 poults	6000
Game strips	500
Equipment	1000
	£17,100
Less sale of game, 1500 birds—	£2250
	= £14,850

Two or three hundred birds are given away to the Guns, tenants, etc., and the total number shot is about eighteen hundred. The cost per bird is about £8. If the owner can get eight Guns paying £1800 each, he should be able to give them ten days' shooting. He can then reckon to keep his shoot going, without making money but without losing much. Normally, of course, he will reserve one or two Guns for himself, for which he must pay.

If a syndicate took this shoot to run themselves, they would have to pay rent and rates. For two thousand acres this might be £5000 – which would mean that the Guns would have to find about £2500 each, and every pheasant they shot would cost about £11.

The value of money has considerably changed since they used to say when a pheasant was shot: 'Up goes a pound, bang goes tuppence, down comes half-a-crown.' The price seems to have gone up to about eight times as much. Costs naturally vary between shoots. One might use estate workers as beaters and not pay them anything extra above their normal wages; another might not buy poults but instead carry out intensive rearing with eggs from their own birds. Some areas are very suitable for wild birds, and no rearing need be done. Plenty of things can upset the calculations – like the very hard winter of 1962–63, or the foot-and-mouth epidemic of 1967–68. Bags may vary considerably. Those of the royal estate at Sandringham have been published and they show such divergences as 16,000 birds shot in 1961–62 and only 2,300 in 1963–64.

Partridge manors are rarely available to syndicates and costs per bird are difficult to calculate, anyway. The amount of shooting that can be done must vary with the survival rate of the chicks during the summer. Grouse moors are let for about £10–£25 per brace of birds they can be expected to provide. An average bag over poor and bad years, with good management, should be one bird to three acres.

On a formal shooting day, as distinct from a walk-round on a rough shoot, many different activities happen at the same time. The man who jumps into game shooting after buying a gun, having a few lessons and then joining a syndicate still has much to learn. The best way for him to find out how a shoot operates is to do some of the essential jobs. A day or two's beating, a day of loading for a friend, and a day with the pickers-up would teach him things he might never learn purely as a Gun. Of course, he may not want to know. But it is the sure way of getting the most out of the sport. To savour it thoroughly, you should understand as much as possible about it. You do not necessarily have to rear a pheasant to understand the problems involved, but you will never fully appreciate what you owe to a keeper unless you visit a summer rearing field at least once. If you have experienced the distances beaters have to walk and the thick, wet cover they must penetrate, you will be more tolerant when waiting at your peg for a drive to begin. If you have been a loader and seen easy birds missed and superb birds cleanly killed, you will know more than most people about the vagaries of other men's performances – points you would miss while busy concentrating on your shooting. Studying style helps to improve your own. (Plates 37, 38.)

The luckiest shooting man is the one who owns a reasonably biddable dog. It does not have to be of Field Trial standard or even guaranteed steady. Steadiness is a prime asset, but when taken picking-up the dog can be kept on a lead during a drive. Nearly all gundogs bred from a working strain have good noses and will retrieve naturally anyway.

Training is needed mainly to control their eagerness. The picker-up's dog must at least answer the call-in whistle and should preferably be trained sufficiently to obey the stop whistle.

It always seems a pity when one sees a dog owner without his dog on an important formal shooting day; he has left it at home because he is unsure of its steadiness. This, of course, is better than bringing the dog, to be a nuisance to himself and his friends, but if unsteadiness is its only major fault, the owner could recompense his dog and enjoy himself too if he took it picking-up on another occasion.

In some syndicates the members have a Gun on some but not all shooting days, according to how much they pay. The non-shooting days are the ones on which to try some of the other jobs on the shoot, and the best of these is picking-up.

During a drive, the picker-up should normally stand back from the Guns – as long as they know where he is. Sometimes, for safety reasons, he has to be up close to the gun-line: but from farther back, he can mark the fall of birds and will often see one which, though hit, flies on strongly and then suddenly collapses. Usually, it is better not to pick up during a drive, but a dog may be put on to a strong runner when there is no likelihood of it chasing off elsewhere. If you are working a partly-trained dog, do not let it loose in the middle of a drive so that it runs forward towards the Guns and then gallops around picking up birds in the open. All dogs like to take the easy ones, but their job is to find the difficult birds. This sounds obvious, but quite a number of Guns who bring dogs with them do no more after a drive than wave an arm vaguely to their dogs and tell them to go and see what they can find – and the dogs go for the game in the open, which a man could collect.

A regular picker-up soon differentiates between the

helpful Guns and the tiresome ones. The good Gun really does mark his birds and makes an effort to describe the fall of the difficult ones. The unhelpful Gun gives a vague indication and goes off to have a chat with his neighbour. He is also the fellow who is apt to have imaginary runners, over which so much time can be wasted. Some Guns do not know that pheasants are naturally reluctant to fly farther than they need. They often stop flapping their wings after they have passed the gunline and glide down towards the nearest cover. The ignorant shooter thinks that the gliding is a sign that he hit the bird, and so he tries to persuade someone to look for it for him.

On the better shoots, a proper 'Plan for the Day' is made, with copies issued to Guns and pickers-up. As well as giving the order of the drives, it may have special instructions for the pickers-up – about staying behind after one drive even when the next has started, for instance. As a picker-up, you must always know where the next drive is and also where you may not take your dog for fear of disturbing game which is due to be dealt with later. Well-organised shoots have a method of announcing the end of a drive: a toot on a horn or a whistle, or just a shout of 'Beaters out!' It certainly helps flank Guns and pickers-up, who may not be able to see what is going on. Good organisation also allows a reasonable time for the pick-up. It is irritating for the keeper and pickers-up if the host insists on quickly bundling the Guns into Land-Rovers and scuttling off to the next stand, where they only sit around gossiping for twenty minutes or more before the first birds can be expected.

Picking-up is excellent experience for young dogs once they have undergone discipline training, but not before. Steadiness can be tested, and checked, by sitting the dog close behind a Gun – with his concurrence, of course. Any tendency to whine will be noticed, but this is generally very difficult to cure. Some dogs go quite wild with excitement when made to sit in the gunline, screeching and howling as if they were being beaten. Attempted cures have included muzzling and even blindfolding, but these restraints fail to muffle the exciting sounds and smells. A dog which behaves really badly in this way will have to be relegated from the formal shooting field to something a bit wilder and rougher.

There is great fascination in seeing one's own dog carry out a good retrieve. Someone has a wing-tipped bird down, which dropped 'over there, by the track along the edge of the plough'. You send out your dog, which gallops over to the plough, hunts along with its nose down and circles back to the track. Pause, much sniffing around and then a hesitating walk down the track, nose to the ground. Then a trot and the dog follows the scent for three or four hundred yards to a junction with a hedge.

'Don't think it went that far', says the man who shot the bird. 'Let's look further up the track.'

You see your dog enter the hedge and work along it. Soon the dog is out of sight. Anxious moments follow: is it coursing a hare into the next county? The Gun wants to move off to the next drive, anyway. Then the dog breaks out of the hedge – with a live pheasant in its mouth. . . .

This is fine when it happens in full view of the field and everyone can see that your dog is all right and knows what its job is. But on other occasions the animal might not bring back a runner quite so quickly. Then you may have to go and investigate. The dog may have marked it to ground in a rabbit hole; or the bird may have managed to fly up a few feet into a small tree. Pheasants have been found in odd places, such as a pig shelter containing several of the rightful occupants. A partridge that fell into an empty five-gallon oil drum posed a problem, only solved when someone went to have a look in the clump of nettles where it had dropped. Except in such unnatural circumstances, a dog with a good nose will bring back a runner eventually. But in the meantime, its anxious owner may have to employ a fair amount of trust and patience.

It is wise to tread warily when picking-up for the first time on a strange shoot. You have to find out the foibles of the host and keeper and learn how they like things run. It is also advisable to avoid caustic comment when somebody else's dog misbehaves. Its owner might well be your host.

What humans define as bad behaviour is very catching among dogs. If you notice a wild dog while you are picking-up – or when you are shooting, for that matter – you should take care to keep your dog away from it in case any of its funny habits are passed on. The safest place for your dog during the lunch break is in the car, where it will not be tempted to get up to any mischief. (Plates 54 and 42.) This lesson was not heeded by a shooting party having lunch in a small barn by a farm. The dogs, normally well behaved, were left sitting outside. Several free-range chickens were scratching around. The sun shone, all was peaceful and the dogs dozed quietly. All at once, the Guns heard a squawk outside and then silence. Nobody paid much attention. But when the squawking was repeated, someone went out to investigate. There were two dead hens lying on the ground and a spaniel was chasing some others. The Gun shouted at the dog and then saw that all the other dogs were on their feet, looking interested. The hens, scattering in front of the spaniel, were passing close to the dogs and as the man turned in the doorway to call his friends from their meal a general chicken-chase began. Soon, each owner was yelling at his

[156]

dog. Some of the men grabbed sticks and ran into the fray. Feathers flew and hens squawked as men swore and dogs ran riot. The mix-up spread out across the fields and it was half an hour before the situation was under control. Seventy hens were killed, and the affair took a bit of explaining to the farmer.

On a big day, several pickers-up can be fully occupied, because when large numbers of birds are shot there are always many that fall well behind the gunline – most of them not accounted for by those who shoot them. A really good hunt through the area yields many birds which would otherwise be lost. Some shoots scarcely bother with pickers-up, or have insufficient. This is a mistake, not only as far as increasing the size of the bag is concerned but also for avoiding unnecessary cruelty to wounded birds.

Here is an example of the value of a man and his dog, even on a small 'cocks only' day late in the season:

Mike, the picker-up, watched the cock-pheasant flinch and continue on set wings across the valley. He marked it into an ivy-clad beech at the edge of a wood, and presently he saw the other picker up go across and put in his dogs. At the end of the drive, Mike and the Gun who had shot the bird joined the search. All three reckoned that the bird had settled in the tree and was probably lying dead at its base; but the dogs disagreed. There was no sign of a fall – no feathers, no line, no bird.

Mike, who believes that the best job in the sporting field is that of huntsman to a pack of foxhounds, decided to 'lift' his labrador bitch and cast her well back in the wood. Perhaps the pheasant had never settled in the tree, and perhaps it was a runner. Eighty yards into the wood, the bitch got her nose down and her movements immediately indicated probable success to her handler. The labrador disappeared

[157]

from sight, but in a couple of minutes she appeared again carrying the live cock.

'Anything doing in there?' shouted the Gun. 'Afraid we'll have to leave it.'

'I've got your bird.'

'Oh, well done.'

Mike felt pleased with his bitch as he came out of the wood, and mentally awarded her a raw egg with the evening meal. The Gun deserved credit too, for he had carefully marked where the bird was last seen and had taken an active interest in trying to find it.

Some Guns might just as well shoot clay pigeons, in Mike's opinion, for all the interest they take in their shots one second afterwards. 'Yes,' said old Ted – who has been beating, picking-up and loading for fifty years – when Mike suggested this theory to him. 'The good 'uns 'll take plenty o' trouble to tell 'ee where their birds are. But some on 'em just bugger off soon's the drive's over. Prob'ly nip back to the Land-Rover for a goo at their flasks. Clay pigeons – hah! You got summat there!'

On the next drive, Mike had to stand close behind the Guns. The ground sloping up behind them would have made it dangerous for him to stand there. A high bird came down the line, was saluted and finally wing-tipped by the Gun on Mike's left. It crashed through a thorn bush behind and landed in a wide dry ditch. It ran. Mike turned to look at his dog and she looked at him. He knew she had seen exactly what had occurred and he gave her 'Hi, lost!' Away she went, straight to the fall, up the overgrown ditch and back with the bird within a minute. 'Good show,' thought Mike. 'That'll save a bit of time at the end.'

He marked another potential runner before the end of the drive – a long shot by No. 1 out on the end of the line. 'Yes,' said No. 1. 'Afraid he's gone through the brambles beyond that holly bush, making for the firs.' It was not difficult. Mike took the bitch to the holly, cast her out, watched for the umpteenth time that magical labrador nose strike it hot and chase up the line to the fir wood. Soon the cock was to hand.

On the first drive after lunch, Mike was leaning over a gate, a ploughed field behind him and a wood a few yards to his right, when a Gun in front dropped a fast, downwind bird which fell behind Mike on the plough. He saw it lying still and turned to look to the front again. Presently, he was aware that the bitch was intently looking behind and was very close to taking off. He spoke to her and looked back, to see that the pheasant had disappeared. Soon the drive ended and he sent the bitch out over the plough, where she took a line across to the wood. He was waiting as she hunted out of sight down the wood when he saw a cock come out a hundred yards away and run across the field. Another bird? If it was the hunted runner, why on earth did it come out of the wood into the open? The first question was soon answered when the labrador ran out of the wood, still on her line, hunted across the plough until she caught sight of the bird, and then collected it in a neat galloping pick-up. It was most impressive and, apart from a broken wing, the cock had not a mark on it – rather different from some of the runners that dogs have to catch in cover and haul out of thick brambles. One can then forgive an unsightly loss of tail feathers!

The last drive was over a small valley with a wood behind. Mike stood at the edge of the wood, towards the left of the line. Several hens came forward; a cock was killed; a cock was missed; and near the end, a fine high cock sailed over the centre of the line. After four shots, it hesitated and dropped into the wood. Mike walked across. When he reached the area of the fall, somebody's dog had run-in and was busying about amongst the undergrowth. He ordered the labrador on and watched, fascinated, as she circled around, found a line and disappeared up the hill towards the back of the wood. Another dog came along and joined the first one in bustling about and not achieving anything, and soon the first dog trotted out of the front of the wood again. Trying not to feel smug, Mike stood still, confident that his dog was on the right line but still prepared to look silly if the dog running around nearby should suddenly pick up a dead cock while his bitch was following an unshot pheasant or even a hare. Two or three minutes of uncertainty went by; and then back came the bitch, carrying the cock. A perfect end to the day.

Mike came out of the wood with the bird. He was not in too much of a hurry to put it in the game cart: might as well let one or two people see that he had got it. Without being unkind to the two dogs which had failed even to find the line of the runner, he was glad to have support for his theory that a working dog must be encouraged to work – which it always will, with enjoyment, when given the chance. It is the neglected dog that tends to dash around letting off surplus energy, picking up easy birds lying in the open, and avoiding the effort of finding difficult birds in thick cover. Its usefulness soon deteriorates.

Mike made no claim that his bitch had a specially good nose : just ordinary gundog scenting powers. Indeed, in his experience, owners who claimed 'a marvellous nose' for their dogs were usually covering up other vices, so that their full claim ought to be something like : 'the dog whines, runs in, fights, chases hares and is hard-mouthed; otherwise it's not too bad and has a good enough nose to follow a runner'.

On this day, Mike's dog had not put a foot wrong. With not a great deal of work to do, as one would expect on a 'cocks only' day late in January, she had nevertheless collected five strong runners out of a total bag of thirty-nine pheasants – which at twelve-and-a-half per cent was a useful proportion. Mike was, of course, lucky in being in the right place to see what was required. And perhaps he was luckier still to have a working dog as a partner. (Plate 63.)

CHAPTER EIGHT

UNUSUAL SHOTS

UNUSUAL shots are often reported in Letters-to-the-Editor columns, sometimes with the query 'Is this a record?' They are usually interesting but rarely instructive. Under the same general heading, one can consider difficult shots and accidental shots – which do not receive the same amount of publicity although there is more likely to be something to learn from them.

An example of a flying shot that had an unusual result concerns a boy who was walking along a lane after a rabbiting expedition. Some partridges suddenly crossed the lane. He fired one shot and killed nine of them. This frightened him, because he was not allowed to shoot game. So he quickly collected the birds and tried to sell them to a dealer. He could not admit to the landowner that he had shot at a partridge and he could not take the birds home, where his father would have been equally angry. But the dealer accused him of having deliberately 'browned' a covey while it was sitting on the ground. and it was difficult to argue his way out of the situation; in fact, he did not get into trouble but he realised that his fluke shot had not been exactly a lucky one for him.

A duffer who hardly ever hit anything and generally missed yards behind *did* manage one lucky if unusual shot. One day he was confronted by a covey flying through a gateway. He fired at the leading bird, missed, and killed all the rest.

There are many right-and-left stories, like the one that records two blackcock with the right barrel and two pigeon with the left. The shooter afterwards said that he must have been seeing double! Various multiple shots have been claimed, often at duck in India or Egypt. Sandgrouse figure in some of these foreign tales, one of which records seven birds to one barrel and five to the other. But high on the list of odd occurrences comes the feat of killing two partridges with the last shot of the day and following this by killing two pheasants with the first shot of the next day.

Some examples of an unexpected addition to the bag concern sitters which were out of sight beyond the bird fired at. One partridge shot flying and a whole covey killed on the ground thirty yards farther on was apparently not so rare in the days of walking-up when the birds were plentiful.

Related in H. S. Gladstone's *Record Bags and Shooting Records* is the Great Shot, when Mr. O'Malley was shooting grouse near the still-famous Ballinahinch salmon fishing in Connemara. He killed his bird and also an unseen hare. But there was more to come. A local who was watching said, 'Begorra, sir, you have made a great shot and have killed a salmon.' The fish was retrieved, and it weighed 10 lbs.

A few years ago a moor in Northumberland had a covey containing two white grouse. Late in the season, when these unusual birds were frequenting the low ground where blackcock were about, one of them was shot; the man who did so had the distinction of killing with consecutive shots a red grouse, a white grouse and a black grouse.

In Chapter Six it was related how a duck fell on a man and knocked him out. The blow received from a falling bird is indeed severe, and high pheasants have broken through

[163]

the tiles of a roof on which they have fallen. Rarer but authenticated occurrences have been a pheasant which fell on a hare and killed it, and a grouse which towered and then fell back on to another grouse, killing it.

A remarkable shot was one made by a very indifferent performer. He was slow and often missed opportunities because he had either forgotten to load his gun or omitted to push off the safety-catch. He rarely shot straight and he was always being chaffed by his friends. But he was a man of good humour and never seemed to mind. One rough-shooting day, while the party was having lunch at a farmhouse, one of them placed a dead rabbit by a hedge in the orchard. When the Guns came out, he said, 'Look at that rabbit, Bill! See if you can hit it.'

Bill loaded his gun, fired, and was delighted when he went up to the rabbit to find it dead. Meanwhile, the farmer had taken the shot out of a cartridge and filled the space with sand. As an afterthought, he put back one pellet. He came up to Bill while the others were congratulating him and said, 'I'll bet you a pound that you can't shoot that white pigeon on the roof.'

'You're on,' replied Bill. 'I'm shooting well now. I can do it.'

'Right. But no second chance, you know. Look, I'll be quite fair. Here's a cartridge. I'll load it for you. Now, show us what you can do.'

Bill took careful aim, fired, and the pigeon rolled down off the roof.

'There you are,' he said. 'Where's my quid? Look, it's shot through the head.'

And it was, too, with that one pellet. Practical jokes do misfire sometimes.

Clay pigeon shooters have made some remarkable scores

[164]

in competition, but one solo performance which captures the imagination is the breaking of 1000 clays in the shortest possible time. In 1957, J. Wheater did this in 42 minutes 22½ seconds, and went on for a full hour to kill a total of 1308 'birds'. Expert clay shots can break five clays thrown into the air at the same moment. It is even more difficult to kill five real pigeon and have them all dead in the air at once, but it has been done.

Three young friends once found a remarkable line for pigeon. Each year for about a fortnight the birds used to flight early in the morning from a wood, on one side of which was a deep valley with a river running along the bottom. The young men had great sport during the thirty minutes that the flight lasted. Then one of them had an idea. 'If we could borrow Mr. Black's five-shot Browning, we might get five birds at one go. They fall down towards the river and if we were lucky someone could get five dead in the air all at once.'

Mr. Black agreed to lend his gun when he had been told about the plan. He said he thought it was possible to kill the fifth bird before the first hit the valley floor, and he suggested that they ought to have a couple of 'official' observers. The best shot took the automatic gun the next morning, but the most he could manage was three birds at one time. The flight was decreasing in size and the project had to be abandoned until the following November.

Next year the friends were eagerly waiting for the pigeon flight to re-establish itself; and sure enough, it did. The same arrangements were made, and on the first morning the best score was only two birds. But the next day, four in a row was achieved twice. The following day two was again the best they could do. But then came a morning of strong wind, against which the birds had to fly. The first attempt was a success – five dead in the air at the same time; and the delighted shooter said he thought he might even have had one or two more if the gun had held more cartridges. For once, the conditions were just right: a steady stream of pigeon with a headwind to slow them down, the gun did not jam and the shooting was straight. The feat was, in fact, repeated ten minutes later; but never again after that.

- Which is the most difficult shot? This is a question often discussed, to which there can be no final answer that would satisfy everyone. Eric Parker in *The Shooting Week-end Book* listed the choice of various pundits who were 'recognised game shots', and all of them were first-class shots as well. Pride of place seems to go to a really high pheasant, thirty-five yards up, gliding with motionless wings and curling in the wind. Following close in degree of difficulty are: a low pheasant which comes straight at you and must be taken behind, against a dark background; driven snipe; jinking woodpigeon; and pochard or tufted duck going downwind.

One's own choice must depend on the type of shooting one most frequently enjoys. The majority of shooters simply do not have the opportunity of judging the respective merits of properly shown high pheasants and grouse swerving round a hillside. But everyone knows one or two types of shot which he finds more difficult than the others. Often, the reason for missing lies not in the bird but in the man behind the gun.

The views of a shooting coach on this subject are that, basically, all shots are difficult if you do not know how to shoot, and all are easy if you do. But that does not mean that no one should ever miss. Everyone does – even shooting coaches. If you watch a good shot, it all looks amazingly easy, just as it does if you see first-class golf, tennis, cricket or show-jumping. The answer is style: all actions performed

[166]

correctly, easily, naturally and apparently without effort. It has been said of many things, from buying a horse to admiring a woman, that one should start at the feet and work up. The same applies to the shooter, whose first task is to adopt a correct stance, as described in Chapter One. From there, correct gun mounting and a relaxed swing must ensure a kill. Theoretically.

What do we do wrong when we miss? All sorts of things. In the field, the most common initial cause of missing is wrong stance and bad footwork. The instructor cannot do much about this except to try to impress on his client its importance. A frequent fault he sees in the school is the lifting of the face from the stock too soon. He calls it 'bird watching', especially on the straight overhead shot when the shooter so often wants to raise his head as he pulls the trigger. 'Have a peep if you must,' he says. 'But you may see more than you expect. Like eavesdroppers who hear more than they want to.'

Another fault is flinching, which is more common than might be supposed. It may be only very slight but it is enough to cause a hesitation to the swing, with results which are fatal to straight shooting but not at all to the bird. Everyone knows most of the standard faults but may be unaware of which one most applies to him. It may be that the diagnosis of a particular fault would help to eliminate a type of difficult shot.

Is it the man or the bird that makes the shot difficult? It's all very well for the instructor to say that all shots are easy if you do the right thing, but many of us consider that cold comfort. We do not find all shots the same. Some *are* more difficult. Circumstances make things less easy: cold, bad light, care needed because of the danger of hitting another person, and so on. When the shooter is in doubt about

[167]

taking a shot, he is almost bound to miss. A relaxed state of body and mind and a carefree attitude are essential, coupled with practised movements that automatically put body, eye and gun in the correct 'groove'.

Assuming we are on form and in a happy frame of mind, the reasons why we miss some shots are as follows. When following with the muzzles the long range or high bird, the movement of the gun tends to be slow and a conscious effort is needed to swing ahead of the bird to give sufficient forward allowance. If the bird is curling in the wind, instead of bringing the gun up through its tail and head, you should swing through the tip of its downwind wing. When a pheasant is gliding, be convinced that it is travelling faster than if its wings were flapping, and increase the lead. Correct 'reading' of the bird will also tell you that it is dropping, and therefore the gun needs to be swung down the bird's line – under its throat and not out over the back of its head, as in the case of a rising pheasant.

A lowish bird comes at you and cannot be taken in front because of safety risks, or because it suddenly appears just over the top of a tree only a few yards in front of you. What often happens is that the shooter hurriedly bangs off one barrel in front of him but two yards behind the pheasant, and then stumbles round with his gun muzzles pointing any old where and brings up the gun for another miss. What should happen is this: the bird is too close to be taken in front and so you are going to take a pace round to the rear, as soon as possible in the gun mounting. You put the muzzles on the bird, butt close to the right forearm, and step round quickly with the left foot ahead of the bird. The muzzles never leave the pheasant's line of flight. Having settled your stance, with your left foot now pointing in the opposite direction to that in which you were originally facing, you

[168]

mount the gun and the muzzles pass *down* the bird's flight line. Swing on, lean forward on the left foot, and fire. The muzzles must be moving down for this shot and the butt must not be at the shoulder as you turn: if it is, you will wobble off the line of your bird and probably still be off balance until it is out of range. If the bird does not come straight over you but is sufficiently out to a flank to be dangerously low, then you should not follow it with the muzzles. Instead, keep the muzzles up and, with your left hand out in front of your face, follow the bird with your left forefinger. (In fact, your finger is out of sight behind the barrels, but that does not matter.) Hang on to the line with the forefinger, and when you mount the gun the muzzles will fall into the line which your eye has never left. (Plate 55.)

The fairly long-range low bird is easily missed, probably because it looks bigger and closer than it would at the same range up in the air. As a high bird it would be given the required forward allowance, but against a background of bushes and trees the shooter misjudges the range and misses behind. In fact, range judging should be easier except when the background is water or mudflats.

Very fast-flying birds, like downwind duck, need fast reactions. First-class shots have extremely quick reactions, and they can read their bird and mount the gun before slower men have even appreciated that they have been offered anything to shoot at. They also have time to move their feet into the correct place instead of shooting from an awkward stance such as that shown in Plate 38. This quick eye and brain is usually a gift and is the mark of the expert in so many sports and games. To a certain extent it can be developed by practice but, like a horseman's hands, it is usually bestowed or withheld at birth.

Woodpigeon can be difficult even for good shots

[169]

who have had very little experience of them. Unlike pheasants and partridges, which mostly fly fairly straight, pigeon take avoiding action as soon as they see a man. The inexpert shot finds that the bird executes its jink just at the instant he fires, and so he knows he has missed as he squeezes the trigger. Pigeon are dealt with by the expert in two ways: one is to remain so well hidden that the bird does not jink; the other is to watch it over the muzzles, let it jink, and then follow it on and shoot.

It seems, then, that the shot defined as 'difficult' is basically the one at which the man who gives it as his choice has not had very much experience. The degree of difficulty is enhanced by anxiety – because this is the shot which he knows is liable to bring failure – and by outside circumstances: if he is cold, his physical movements will be slower; and if he is wondering about safety, doubt will cause delay and then a fruitless poke. The difficulty may also be increased because an inherent fault in the shooter's style is emphasised. He may get away with genuinely easy shots, but the others show up his moderate technique. (Plate 62.)

The bird on the right, which is not of itself a difficult shot, is often missed because of poor technique. The shooter transfers his weight from the left to the right foot, or lets his left hip stick out. The effect is to drop the right shoulder, cant the barrels and miss below. The cure is to reach up and push the gun out and up, keeping the weight on the left foot and the shoulders square. The shoulder should follow in to the butt, and he should not pull the butt back into his shoulder. The barrels then remain horizontal and in line with the bird's flight path.

What is an easy shot, anyway? Many people find all sorts of shots easy – to miss. A slow, low close-range shot, such as a pigeon battling against the wind or an unfrightened hare trotting along, ought to be dead easy. But it is often missed because we count it in the bag before we have gone through the motions of mounting the gun properly. We just fire at it with no vestige of a swing. We are frightened of missing in front. Shooting *at* any moving target is the greatest cause of misses. At the risk of tiresome repetition, you are asked again always to read your bird, pick it up over the muzzles and follow it with eye and body, and only *then* bring the butt to your shoulder. This basic technique is what makes difficult shots easy – after you have had a great deal of practice.

A pigeon shooter once stood on a corner of a wood round which pigeon were flighting very fast downwind, making for their roosting wood a quarter of a mile behind him. The farmer came along to watch and was astonished at the skill of the shooter. Bird after bird was killed. The farmer congratulated the shooter and asked him to come again the next evening. But on the following day the wind had changed, and the pigeon were coming over very high and then dropping down quickly to roost. The shooter went inside their wood and the birds came flapping in against the wind, almost hovering like butterflies. They were too easy, he thought, as he shot more or less straight at them. But it took him a box of cartridges before he hit one. The farmer was laughing at him and, in desperation, he started to swing through the birds properly. After that, he killed a couple of dozen with hardly any misses.

Sometimes, when you have experienced a whole row of misses, it seems as if the unusual shot is the one that eventually connects. 'What on earth did I do then?' you ask yourself, as the bird obligingly falls to the ground. Try to analyse your actions and you will undoubtedly find that you simply followed the correct drill – from collecting the bird over the muzzles to swinging through and keeping your cheek glued to the stock.

Really easy shots are not worth taking, anyway. An unpleasant piece of showing-off occurred when a party of youngsters were returning from snipe-shooting over a marsh. About a hundred golden plover came over two or three gunshots high. 'Watch this,' said one fellow, and fired at them. The plover promptly dived almost to ground level, as these birds often will, flattened out and sped by. He shot into the middle of them with his second barrel and knocked down fifteen. An easy shot, but hardly a satisfactory one.

Trick shots or too-clever shots should never be attempted at living creatures. Even the joke of snatching someone's hat, throwing it into the air and drilling it to look like a colander is foolishly dangerous. If you play carelessly with a gun, someone is liable to be hurt. A clever bit of shooting is to shoot the shot charge off a cartridge. With the gun in the left hand, this is achieved by holding the cartridge in the right hand, throwing it up in the air and then shooting so precisely that the limited pattern spread at so short a range removes the complete shot charge. The powder charge and the brass end are left unmarked. It demands accurate shooting and timing. Judgement of the exact range at which to fire is vital. If the target is too close or too far away it will be missed, or the whole of it will be hit. There is no danger in this trick shot, provided normal safety precautions are taken: a clear area in front of the shooter, and any spectators keeping behind him.

Accidental shots have marred the sport of shotgun shooting ever since it began, which in England was soon after the Restoration in 1660. Shooting flying—an import from France – became a fashion among the gentry and, indeed, almost a cult. It was a difficult sport, to hit a bird on the wing, quite different from shooting sitting birds for food, the normal procedure previously. The Gunmakers Company of London had been entrusted with the proof-firing of barrels in 1637; in 1672, when bursting barrels on sporting flintlocks were causing casualties among sportsmen, the sale of unproved barrels was prohibited and the Company was granted a charter which allowed it to set the standard of proof. This was a help in reducing accidents but it did not prevent careless behaviour, which still goes on. A record from those days describes how a gentleman was out practising pistol shooting. It was well known that if rain entered the flashpan of a flintlock it wet the priming and normally prevented the weapon from firing, so when a storm burst upon this gallant he flung a loaded pistol on the ground in disgust and ran for shelter. The pistol went off and shot his servant in the leg.

Advice about the safe handling of guns was given in Chapter Five. Do not shoot where you cannot be sure of the effect of the shot. Perhaps we become tired of being told this when we know we are never guilty of such behaviour. But some people are. A recent newspaper report describes how two men were out trying to shoot foxes. One was shot in the head. The other said afterwards: 'I saw a movement in a ditch and just let fly. I thought it was a fox but it was my pal's brown cap.' Perhaps we should not be too smug about those garish clothes we hear are worn by 'hunters' in America in order not to be mistaken for foxes, deer or anything else on the game licence.

A party were out ferreting. One of them saw what he thought was a rabbit moving through the brambles on top of a bank. He fired – and hit the head of a boy who was walking along the other side of the bank.

When there are Guns walking with beaters extra care is needed. No one likes to hear an unruly crowd of shouting beaters, and well-drilled professionals move about their busi-

[173]

ness with plenty of stick-tapping and an occasional whistle or 'Brr-brr'. It is important that they should make some noise, for safety reasons. If a laggard slopes along with his hands in his pockets, picking an easy path and lost in thought, he may get shot. A walking Gun could reasonably turn round to take a bird breaking back, or even a hare, and the poor beater, unseen behind a bush, will be on the receiving end. Whose fault is it? The Gun is only slightly blameworthy. It is really the beater's own fault.

But would the host and the keeper be satisfied in their minds that it was not largely *their* fault for not ensuring that all the beaters knew exactly how to behave?

A shot that accidently wounds a man is not always fired carelessly. On one shooting party a hare came between the walking-up line of Guns. Two of them turned to watch it and one said, 'Yours, Tom.' The other waited until it was well back and fired as it crossed a small stream, whereupon his neighbour jumped 'higher than I've ever seen a standing man jump before', as another in the party said later. The wounded man only remembered coming down and being knocked over. He was severely hit about the legs and several pellets had to be extracted in hospital, but he luckily suffered no permanent injury. The shot had ricocheted from a slate slab sticking up unseen in the stream bed. This was a pure accident, very upsetting for the friend who caused it.

Guns are dangerous. If people would never lose sight of this, there might be fewer accidents. The trouble is that most dangerous shots, who do not quite hit somebody but teeter on the verge of doing so, are virtually incurable. The only defence is to refuse to shoot with them again, once having seen their behaviour. The self-description 'safe shot' should never be accepted at face value.

An acquaintance was walking down a ride with his gun

under his arm. Suddenly, there was an explosion and the shot from one of his barrels ploughed a furrow in the ground three yards to the side of a beater. 'I was just going to unload,' he said. 'Must have left the safety-catch off at the end of the last drive.' Astonishingly, many shooters adopt a casual attitude towards the safety-catch. Another fellow explained how he had missed an opportunity: 'We'd walked up that field without seeing a thing. At the end I was going along by the hedge towards the gate, and right in the corner a cock pheasant got up at my feet. I swung on to him, pulled the trigger and nothing happened. Of course, I'd put my safety-catch back on and the gun wouldn't fire. Wasn't that rotten luck?' If the safety-catch is to mean anything at all, it must always be on until the moment of firing.

The accident that this man could have caused would have been of the type when, through carelessness, the gun goes off unexpectedly. The other type, when the gun is fired deliberately but in a careless manner, is more common. It is never worth the risk to fire at a hare in front, or at a pheasant below the tops of the trees, when waiting for beaters to approach through a covert. Better to remember Mark Beaufoy's celebrated verses to his son which end: 'All the pheasants ever bred, won't repay for one man dead.' It is a pity that hosts and syndicate leaders are no longer authoritarian, as in the days when dangerous shooting was punished by the culprit being sent home. Even in today's permissive society, it would be sensible if the man in charge of the shoot has a quiet word with the offender at the first opportunity. If the latter turns truculent, there is no wise alternative to ensuring that he visits the shoot no more.

Accidental shots can take a slightly amusing turn, tempered with the knowledge that the comedy might have been tragedy. A man took a shot at a low bird flying along a hedge. When he went through the gate a little later he found a farm tractor the other side of the hedge; it had been shot in the radiator and was sadly spewing water. Perhaps he learnt something from the incident.

On another occasion two friends agreed to meet in a certain wood for pigeon flighting. They were both keen young novices, and one of them arrived early. He climbed up some of the trees and fixed decoys in them, and then he thought he would be closer to the pigeons when they arrived if he stayed up in a tree, especially as he found one covered in ivy in which he could hide. The second lad came into the wood, mistook the decoys for real pigeons and began to stalk them. When he heard a rustling in the ivy-covered tree he thought it must be a pigeon and so he fired at it. Down fell his pal! They had to go to a doctor where the victim's injuries were found to be surprisingly trivial. Later, being young, they laughed about it; but they were both very lucky.

Game shooting can hardly be called a dangerous sport, but accidents are by no means rare. It is advisable, therefore, to take out an insurance policy for public liability against accident. The premium should be not more than about £5.

CHAPTER NINE

THE LAW

THE laws on shooting are not as harsh as the old hunting laws introduced by William the Conqueror, but they are rather more complicated. William helped himself to whatever land he wanted, cultivated or not, and proclaimed it a royal hunting forest. The laws made for the protection of these forests, and the game they contained, were barbarously severe. Punishments involved mutilation; and in William Rufus's reign, the penalty for killing a deer was death. The poorest rustics went on poaching, however, in order to obtain food. They used the longbow and the crossbow, and the chief quarry was deer.

By the beginning of the sixteenth century, fowling-pieces were being used to shoot both birds and beasts. They were matchlocks and were used only for sitting shots. But they were so popular that the longbow, so instrumental in the victorious battles of Agincourt and Crécy, became neglected. In 1508, an Act of Parliament forbade the use of guns or crossbows without a licence – and that was the beginning of shooting legislation as we know it today. Nobody paid much attention to this Act, nor to one in 1511 which demanded that every Englishman under the age of forty should possess a longbow and practise with it.

In 1515, a new Act outlawed guns and crossbows except in the hands of those who possessed lands bringing in a yearly income of £200. The effect of this was to make shooting a monopoly of the rich, even when the income clause was reduced to £100 in 1542. By the later statute, hunting or shooting any bird or animal was forbidden for everyone except by royal licence. This first game licence cost £20, in the form of a deposit which could be forfeited for non-compliance with the game laws.

There have, in fact, been numerous game and land laws since the days of King Alfred. Many of them were disregarded in Tudor times. It is interesting to note, however, that the purpose of some of the new laws was not only to preserve the best shooting for the nobility and wealthier squires but also to persuade sportsmen to use weapons thought to be suitable for war. A law of 1549 deplored the use of what we would call scatter-guns because the hail of shot reduced the need for marksmanship required in soldiers; it stated that no one below the rank of lord should shoot more than one pellet at a time. Not that the prohibition made much difference. New laws have continually been made ever since, defining species of game and the periods of the year and times of day when it may be shot; detailing penalties for poaching and for taking the eggs of game birds; even establishing such oddities as the number of pigeon which could legally be shot off a church steeple by one man during a morning. As long as there were no worshippers inside, he was allowed six birds. The present-day laws governing shooting have four main objectives: the conservation of birds and animals; the support of the rights of those who own or rent land; the protection of gun owners from accidents; and assistance to the police in apprehending armed criminals.

Laws now control what we may shoot, when, where and what with. Concerning 'what with', the law's idea of a shotgun is a smooth-bore weapon with a barrel length of not less than 24 inches. Sawn-off shotguns with very short barrels are sometimes used by bank robbers, and they are illegal. Other firearms which may be owned by the public are rifles and revolvers, for which a special certificate is required. The certificate, in 1980, costs £25 and is not easily obtained. You have to give the police some sound reasons for wanting to keep one of these firearms. The owner of a shotgun also needs a certificate, which is normally obtainable from the police without much difficulty (see Appendix F).

The law concerning the possession of guns is in the Firearms Act, 1968. This is rather more concerned with firearms as used by criminals than shotguns as used by sportsmen, but there are still a good many relevant points. A police constable is given powers to search a car for a gun if he thinks an offence has been committed. He may also demand to see your shotgun certificate, and he can seize and detain the gun if you have no certificate. It is an offence, incidentally, to refuse to give one's name and address to the police or to give a false one. The maximum punishment for not having a shotgun certificate is six months in prison or a £200 fine. This also applies to the offence of not complying with the conditions under which the certificate was issued, one of which is that the gun and ammunition must be kept in a secure place; not, for instance, in an unlocked car. It is essential to read what is written on the back of the certificate, where it states that the police must be informed if the gun is lost or stolen.

The law is strict about the use of guns by young people (see Appendix E). An adult who is supervising a boy is responsible for any 'improper use' of a gun. So if a lad breaks the insulators on the telephone wires with an airgun, whoever was supervising could be fined £50. And the same goes for potting at the neighbour's cat or breaking the windows of his greenhouse.

New shotguns have to be subjected to a proof test before they are sold. Old guns may become out of proof for a variety of reasons (see Appendix A). It is an offence to sell or exchange a gun which is out of proof.

'What' you may shoot is loosely thought of as game, which is usually preserved and protected by a close season; wild-fowl, which are 'free' but also have seasons; and vermin, which may be shot at any time as long as the shooter is authorised – meaning that he has the sporting rights over the land or permission from whoever does own them.

The Protection of Birds Act, 1954 (see Appendix G), contains a great deal of legislation not directly affecting shooting. It covers the protection of birds' nests and their eggs, restrictions on the sale of wild birds, and the sizes of birdcages, etc. The important Schedules for the shooting man are the First – birds protected by special penalties; the Second – those which may be killed at any time; and the Third – those which may be killed except in their close season. The initial effect of the Act is that all wild birds are protected; but then it goes on to say which ones may be killed. Numerous Orders were made under the Act. The result of some of them has been to switch a bird from one Schedule to another, or to vary its status in a particular county.

In 1967 came an amending Protection of Birds Act. There were two important sections: one prohibiting the sale of dead wild geese, and the other allowing the Secretary of State to declare a special protection period in times of severe weather conditions; this could be done outside the close season and was designed to help wildfowl in a very hard winter.

Changes are made from time to time in the details of these Acts: and their jurisdiction is not the same in all parts of Great Britain. For instance, the collared dove – which first appeared here in 1952 and is now quite common – may be killed in Scotland at any time but it used to be protected in England and Wales. Nowadays, however, it may be shot in these countries too. But unless you *know* you are allowed to shoot a bird, you must assume that you are not. All birds of prey are protected, for example, many of them by special penalties. A particular feature of these Acts of 1954 and 1967 is that they do not apply to game birds except in making illegal certain methods of trapping, poisoning and netting them.

The definition of game, when it may be shot, and by whom, is complicated. There are references in the Night Poaching Acts, 1828 and 1844; the Game Act, 1831; the Game Licences Act, 1860; the Hares Act, 1848; the Poaching Prevention Act, 1862, and the Ground Game Act, 1880. Game birds are considered to be pheasant, partridge, grouse, blackgame and, in Scotland, ptarmigan. A game licence is required to shoot these, and also woodcock and snipe. Hares are game and cannot be classified as vermin; a licence is required to shoot them by all but the owner and occupier of land and one other person authorised by him in writing. Rabbits are usually considered to be vermin; nevertheless, a game licence is needed in certain circumstances. The Game Licences Act, 1860, says that a person who kills or takes rabbits must have a licence, but among the exceptions are the owner or tenant of the land and anyone who has his permission. The effect of this is that a trespasser or poacher who kills rabbits should have a game licence. As he almost certainly will not have one, this is another offence with which he can be charged.

[181]

Woodpigeon and stock-doves may be shot, but not tame or racing pigeons. A pigeon which has gone feral may be shot; but if you shoot someone's tame bird, it is no defence to say afterwards that you thought it was a wild one.

Another problem in law is what you may shoot not for sport but to protect your stock. Can you shoot somebody's uncontrolled dog that comes on to your land, or that over which you have the shooting rights, and chases and kills the game on it? The Malicious Damage Act, 1861, makes it an offence to kill or wound 'unlawfully and maliciously' any bird or animal normally kept in confinement or for a domestic purpose. One might think that to shoot a dog chasing game is not unlawful and malicious if there is no other way of stopping it damaging one's property. For instance, a farmer who finds a dog chasing his sheep would surely be justified in shooting it if that was the only way in which he could protect his flock. Sheep-worrying can cause immense damage, especially in the lambing season, and a dog which has formed this habit is usually incurable. But the crucial point is that although the sheep are the farmer's property the game on the land is not his or anyone else's. The owner of the shooting rights may kill the game, and when dead it is his property. He can protect it, and anybody who takes it is guilty of theft. Pheasants in pens for breeding purposes – or young birds also penned – belong to an owner, just like domestic chickens. But when the game birds are turned out into the coverts, they cease to belong to anyone in the legal sense. Therefore you cannot shoot a dog which is chasing game, in order to protect your property, because the game does not, in fact, belong to you. The only remedy is to catch the dog, shut it up, and then claim damages when the owner comes to collect it. The dog's owner can also be sued for trespass if it can be shown that the animal was in the habit of trespassing.

A similar ruling would apply to the shooting of a domestic cat – except that the cat is better protected than the dog in that the law of trespass does not apply, even if the cat was in the habit of coming into your garden and slaying the fantail pigeons as they strutted about the lawn.

'When' you may shoot various creatures is controlled by their close seasons, when they are breeding. See Appendix G for birds. Hares have no close season on ordinary farmland, but they may not be sold while they are breeding – from March to July, inclusive. No game may be shot on Sundays and Christmas Day, and this rule includes hares. The occupier of moorlands and unenclosed lands and persons authorised by him are allowed to shoot ground game (hares and rabbits) only between December 11th and March 31st.

Night shooting of game is illegal, the legal definition of night being between the first hour after sunset and the last hour before sunrise. In Scotland, you may not shoot any wild bird on a Sunday, although in England and Wales you may shoot pigeon and wildfowl in most areas but not all. In certain areas, the killing of birds on a Sunday has been prohibited. If in doubt about a particular locality, you should ask the police there for a ruling.

'Where' you may shoot is governed by permission obtained, or by right of ownership, or by the renting of shooting rights. You might be given permission by a landowner or tenant to shoot on his land, but only at specific things. You must know what sporting rights have been let with any land over which you, as a friend of the tenant, propose to shoot. Game rights would not include wildfowl, but exclusive rights would. The exclusive rights over commonland are normally vested in the lord of the manor. Some owners of commons do not object to local people shooting pigeon and rabbits on their land, but the shooters have no legal right to do so. If commonland adjoins a river, the public could be allowed to shoot duck along the river unless the exclusive sporting rights had been let. If only the game rights had been let, you could shoot duck there even if the lessee had bred duck and turned them down on the river. They would be *ferae naturae* and no longer the property of the man who bred them, like the pheasants chased by the dog mentioned earlier.

The public have no legal right to shoot on the foreshore. This was discussed in Chapter Six. In Scotland, however, shooting on the foreshore is permitted except on nature reserves. In England, a landowner holds the shooting rights unless he has signed them over to a tenant, but in Scotland the opposite applies: the tenant has the rights unless they have been reserved by the landlord.

Although game may not legally be sold during the close season, it is not an offence to possess dead game then, provided that it was killed during the shooting season. This means that it is not unlawful to keep game in a deep freeze for eating during the summer.

Game licences are not cheap, especially for young shots who already find the expense of buying cartridges bad enough. But everyone accepts that in these restriction-ridden times we have to buy licences to do almost everything, except ride a bike or keep a cat. So if you want to shoot game, you must pay the price of a licence.

As well as laws on shooting, there are certain principles which should be followed. Some of these, concerning politeness to one's companions, were mentioned in Chapter Three. The following points of etiquette need attention, too, for safety and to help other shooters and all who enjoy the countryside.

[184]

Keep quiet when game is near. If you talk during a drive, the birds – particularly partridges – will hear you and run unseen out to a flank.

Make a mental note of the birds you kill and where they fall. Try to account for each one after the drive and, if you have no dog, tell the keeper or a picker-up about any genuine runners.

If you make a mistake, like shooting a hen pheasant on a cocks-only day, apologise to your host. He will not mind anything like as much as if he later finds out that you are one of those people who can never admit being wrong.

Check exactly where other Guns are if they are out of sight behind a hedge. And when you are placed by a numbered peg, stay near it. It is bad manners to move to another position where you think you may have better shooting – and you may also place yourself in danger of being shot.

Always have a good look round while waiting for a drive to begin, to see where the stops and pickers-up are.

Carry your gun open, so that your friends can see that it is unloaded. In wet weather, carry it closed with the barrels over your shoulder and the trigger-guard uppermost. Never hold a closed gun over your forearm with the muzzles pointing down at other men's feet or at their dogs. You want to be known as a safe chap to have around, not someone to beware of because his gun is often pointing in a dangerous direction.

Speak well of the day, even if you are feeling a little sad because you have shot badly. Remember that shooting is a sport and for fun, and that it is up to you to see that your companions have a happy day.

Learn the proper way to kill wounded game and always make every effort to find anything you have wounded, even if it means a delay before you can go on shooting. An easy way to kill a wounded bird is to grasp it with both hands, breast uppermost and with its wings held in to its body, and then rap the back of its head smartly on a stone or against a tree or post. To kill a hare, pick it up in your left hand by the small of its back and chop it smartly with the edge of your hand across the back of its neck. With a rabbit, hold it too with the left-hand grip, and break its neck by putting your right hand across the back of its neck and pushing down and away from you.

If you have to cross someone else's land to reach your shooting, ask permission first. Open gates rather than climb them, which strains the hinges. Do not break gaps through hedges, or chop them about indiscriminately when making a pigeon hide. Always pick up litter after a lunch break, particularly bottles and tins. If you have ever seen a dog with a leg slashed on broken glass, you will know the importance of this.

Warn the farmer that you are coming before you visit his land, even if you do have the shooting rights. His goodwill is invaluable and without it you will be severely handicapped.

Co-operate with other people who use the countryside for different sports such as hunting, coursing and fishing. There is room for all, but a positive effort to maintain good relations is needed. As far as your own sport is concerned, keep to the rules and you will always be welcome even if you are only an average shot – which is better than being a super-shot with no thought for others.

CHAPTER TEN

OUT OF SEASON

WHEN the season for game and wildfowl is over, some people put away their guns until the next one begins. Those who do a lot of shooting have their guns overhauled while they take up summer interests. But no one should start a new season without having handled his gun at all in the meantime. The quick way to get some practice is to have a session at a shooting school in the late summer, and many people do this – even those who are considered good enough shots not to need any more lessons.

You may want to keep your hand in and go on learning throughout the close season. Clay pigeon shooting helps, and even if you do not want to take it up as a full-time sport you can have a go at some of the competitions organised by small gun clubs. These are advertised in the local press and the entrance fees are reasonably small. Here you will find good and bad shots, and you can watch their style and try to improve your own.

In the past, a glass-fronted cupboard was recommended for storage of guns where they could be seen and examined, but because of the increasing number of burglaries, it is better nowadays to keep guns out of sight, preferably in a steel cabinet, with the fore-ends stored separately.

If you are still learning to shoot, the more you handle the gun the better. Take it out into the garden, weigh it in your hands and get the feel of it. Put the muzzles on to any bird flying by and practise swinging through it. Check your

[187]

stance and the movements of your feet for taking a shot behind. Make sure that the butt is well into your shoulder and the comb pressed against your cheek.

It is better still, of course, to do some actual shooting during the summer, and this usually means pigeon. Where game is preserved, you will probably not be allowed to shoot from April to July; but you should be able to get permission to shoot pigeon on the newly-sown corn in March, or when they are flighting into the woods to roost. And in August, the keeper will probably let you shoot them when they are feeding on the growing corn. On non-keepered land, you may be allowed to shoot pigeon all the year round.

If you are going to make the most of opportunities for pigeon shooting, you should equip yourself with a portable hide and some decoys. The hide can consist of half a dozen metal rods driven into the ground, on to which you will hang camouflage netting. Or you can use a roll of wire-netting supported on sticks, preferably bamboo for lightness. Tie to the inside of the wire some sacking dyed in patches of brown and green, and through the outside meshes you can push handfuls of grass or whatever is handy when you set it up. (Plate 59.) The sticks will need pegs and simple guy-ropes of string to hold them erect. The hide should be not more than about 4 ft. 6 in. high, so that you can shoot sitting down, probably on a five-gallon oil drum. From this position, you ought to be able to shoot birds attracted to your decoys without the birds seeing you – which is half the battle. Once a pigeon has been alarmed, done a quick jink and accelerated away, it becomes a more difficult shot for the non-expert. Do not forget to have a small sack in the hide to put the dead birds in and, during warm weather, an aerosol fly-killer to squirt into it. In order to conceal your face and neck, you will need a hat with an all-round brim.

For successful pigeon forays, you will have to learn about flight lines and the correct sighting of hides according to the wind, and a good deal more. It would be sensible to read one of the books devoted to this gratifying sport (see Appendix J). Pigeon can provide most testing shooting, and game shots who are good at pheasants – which fly more or less in a straight line – are sometimes perplexed by the pigeon's clever aerobatics. Incidentally, the belief that pigeon are tough and resistant to shot is not true. It arises from the fact that their feathers are very loose and easily come out. If you shoot at one and it flies on, leaving a few feathers in the air, do not imagine that you hit it fair and square. The bird was really right at the edge of the shot pattern and probably only one pellet grazed its body and knocked out a few feathers. One simple point about siting pigeon hides correctly is to put them in the shade, along the south side of the field: not because you may be hot sitting in the August sun but because your movements will show up so much more if you are in the bright light. And pigeon have very sharp eyes.

While you are sitting in your hide, waiting for the pigeon to appear, it is useful practice to mount the gun at some other bird that obligingly flies past: a rook, or a plover, or even a starling. Swing on to it and say to yourself 'Now !' when you would have pulled the trigger ; and make sure that you did not check the swing. If a vermin bird comes along – a crow, or a jay, or magpie – shoot it. They steal other birds' eggs and generally do more harm than good.

Decoys are almost essential for making a good bag of pigeon, and often for making any bag at all if you have not positioned yourself in the right place. You can buy them or make them, and there are many 'recipes' for their construction. Some are made of rubber, some of wood, and others

[189]

of tin, cardboard or even old gumboots. If you make your own, be sure to use matt paint with no hint of any shine in it. The best decoy is the real dead bird, with its head propped up on a piece of stick under its throat. You can put some of these out among the artificial decoys as you shoot them; but in the summer you will lose them as an edible part of the bag, because the flies will spoil them. (Plate 60.)

An improvement on simply having the dead bird lying on the ground is to impale it, per rectum, on a pencil-thin, flexible stick about 3ft long. The point of the stick goes right up inside the pigeon to its head. The other end of the stick is pushed into the ground. Now plant two more 3ft sticks, vertically, about 6ft to each side of the bird; extend its wings and tie the tip of each with thin string or fishing nylon to the vertical sticks. The pigeon is then in a flying position, apparently about to land among the decoys.

Dead birds can be made into more permanent decoys by injecting them with formaldehyde (formalin). A thirty-per-cent solution is required, in the throw-away type of hypodermic syringe supplied to doctors and veterinary surgeons, who will usually give them away after use. A complicated but very efficient method of preparing the bird involves removing most of the body from inside the skin and inserting cotton wool and wire as a support. The lazy way is to remove nothing but simply squirt formalin in all over. A compromise, which saves wasting meat, is to remove the legs, make a cut through the skin from the crop to the vent, take out the internal organs and slice off each breast. (Archie Coats' book, *Pigeon Shooting*, gives excellent recipes for devilling breasts and for making pâté and terrine with them.) Then push cotton wool into the rib cage and place a pad of it where each breast was. Sew up the skin with strong cotton. Now inject the formalin into the back of the skull, the wing muscles, the neck and down the back. Cut off the eyelids and put the bird on a shelf, supported by crumpled newspaper, with its head up, wings in the right place and tail feathers nicely spread out. It will take a week or two to harden. These decoys are cheap to make but need to be looked after carefully, otherwise the feathers will be spoilt. Spraying with hair-lacquer helps to make them last a bit longer.

For successful decoying, you need plenty of the artificials. Two or three are not much good. A dozen is the least number likely to be really effective, and twenty is better still. The decoys ought to be light and strong and unaffected by rain. Some of them should move in the wind as if they were feeding. Cheapness is an advantage, of course, and the answer to all these problems is to use old gumboots as the basic material. One pair will make four decoys, each boot producing one 'sitter' and one 'feeder'. Enquiries among farmers will usually produce boots which have been discarded because of leaks in the foot although the upper remains sound enough. To make a pair of decoys, first clean a gumboot and then mark out on it in pencil the outline shown in Plate 57. The rubber can be cut with strong scissors, but tinsnips are better.

When the patterns have been cut out and laid flat, it will be seen that each bird has a flap on each side below its head. Fold these flaps, one across the other, and stick with a waterproof glue such as Durofix or Uhu. Each decoy will then assume a round shape across its back. Stick the two sides of the head and beak of the 'sitter' together: clothes pegs can be used to hold the pieces while the glue sets. The decoys are now ready for painting.

Matt paint is necessary and the colours needed are black, white, grey and pink, with perhaps a little yellow for the beak and the surround of the eye. The pink is dirtied with grey to form the colour of the breast. Before painting, it is best to get a real dead pigeon – not someone else's decoy – and copy the shades of colour from it. Also check the overall size of the real bird and crop off a little of your decoy if you have been using large-size gumboots. Do not try to be too artistic in the painting: a real bird does not have firmly divided lines of black, white and grey, for the feathers smudge the colours together.

The 'feeder' decoy should have a hollow-nosed rivet or cobbler's eyelet fitted in its back, in such a position that when supported there it assumes a slightly nose-down attitude. Cut a stick about seven inches long, sharpen one end and push a piece of wire into the other, leaving about an inch protruding. Put the stick in the ground and mount the decoy on it, with the wire in the rivet. The decoy will then bob up and down in the wind. If you twist a piece of wire on to the top of the stick so that it points out horizontally through the gap where the throat is, it will stop the decoy from swinging round. If the horizontal wire is a nuisance to carry because it bends or breaks in the bag, it may be dispensed with and the decoy can be kept head to wind with judiciously placed stones. The 'sitter' will be natural enough on longish grass, clover, or stubble, but on short grass it could be lifted slightly on a stone or a short stick.

One pair of gumboots: four decoys. Collect another couple of pairs and you have your dozen – impervious to wet, light and easily carried, and near-enough indestructible.

Those who look after their own shoot will be dealing with vermin during the close season, and decoys can also help here. Crows are acknowledged to be very wily and it is not easy to stalk one and get a shot at it approaching or leaving its nest. A gamekeeper who is out on the ground all the time and knows the birds' habits can sometimes succeed. But if you are in a hide, you may be able to decoy a crow into range.

It is a characteristic of black birds – crows, rooks and jackdaws – to be attracted by something black, probably mistaking it for one of their own species even if the object is not in the shape of a bird. That outstanding naturalist Konrad Lorenz recorded in his book *King Solomon's Ring* the habits of a colony of jackdaws which lived around his house. They were free-flying but very tame. One day, when Lorenz approached the loft where they lived, he had in his pocket a pair of black bathing trunks. He had just returned from a swim and the trunks were wet, so he pulled them out. Immediately, the jackdaws, who knew him well, surrounded him and pecked frantically at his hand. There have been other cases of people being mobbed while carrying some black object.

The best decoy for crows is a dead bird; but until you have shot one, a simple dummy can be made of a small log of wood wrapped with rags, the outside one being black with a couple of ends flapping loosely. The dummy or real corpse is tied to a piece of elastic rubber, the other end of which is fixed to a peg in the ground. One end of a long piece of string is also tied to the dummy and the other end leads back to your hide. If you pull the string, the decoy moves along the ground towards you; and when you suddenly let go, the elastic jerks it back two or three yards. This is a fairly certain draw to any crow flying past just out of gunshot range.

If you set up an owl decoy in the open it will be mobbed by all sorts of birds, and may provide the opportunity to shoot a jay or magpie. A good one is supplied by Cogswell and Harrison of Piccadilly. Ferret-owners sometimes tether one of their animals, with the same idea in mind. It is against the law, however, to use a live bird in this way. Any decoy that moves is more effective than a stationary one and a flapping pigeon decoy is a good addition to the layout of ordinary ones.

Some ingenious mechanical decoys have been made but they are usually fairly complicated and include various pulleys and crank mechanisms. A simple 'flapper' can be constructed as follows:

The first requirement is a solid decoy, preferably carved out of wood. It need not be a work of art and can be fairly roughly hewn, using a real pigeon as model for size and colouring when painting (or you can buy one in the gun shops). In any case, one or two such solid decoys ought to be in the pigeon shooter's equipment for sitting on fence posts and water troughs and for lofting in trees.

The wings are cut out of talc such as is used for map-board covers, and it is roughened with sandpaper to give a matt surface before being painted. Again, a real bird's wings should be copied in order to obtain the right size, shape and colouring. The two wings, outstretched, are in one piece with a straight piece about three inches long joining them in the middle. Under the wings is fixed a strip of flat, springy steel such as is used as bands for securing packing cases. Brass paper-fasteners provide a simple way of securing steel to talc.

The wings are held across the back of the decoy with elastic bands – one round its neck and one under the rear part of its body. The fact that the decoy now has two pairs of wings, one tucked into its sides in the resting position and one pair outstretched, can be ignored.

The decoy has a hole in its base so that it can sit on a stick about three feet long, pushed into the ground. Each end of a short piece of string is tied near the two wingtips. From its centre, another string goes down the stick through a couple of screw eyelets – and this string is about thirty yards long, to reach the shooter's hide. When the long string is pulled, the wingtips bend down. With the string released, the steel strip beneath the wings flips them up again. Owing to the friction of the long length of string across the ground, however, the steel strip alone is not strong enough to pull back the string. So at the base of the stick, tie one end of about eighteen inches of catapult elastic, the other end of which is tied to the string. The elastic pulls the released string back through the grass or stubble and the steel strip is free to flip up the wings.

A word of warning about the long length of string: coil it round a piece of cardboard or a block of wood by revolving the cardboard, *not* by holding the cardboard and twisting the string round it. Every time you coil the string round the cardboard you put in a twist which can cause terrible tangles when you have thirty yards of it out over rough grass – especially in wet weather.

A few quick jerks on the end of the string in the hide will make the 'flapper' work in a remarkably realistic way. Its cost of production is very small and its making involves no difficulties requiring an engineer's work-bench. The satisfaction of success with your own decoy rather than using a ready-made job is akin to catching a trout on a home-tied fly or shooting with self-loaded cartridges – although the skill required for those tasks is a good deal greater than that called for in making this eye-catching decoy. (Plate 58.)

During the summer, there will be plans to make before the season starts. Fixing the dates of the shooting days reasonably early helps everyone concerned. On a pheasant shoot, particularly, a big day fairly early should ensure that a good market is obtained for the birds. As the season progresses, the price drops. On a syndicate shoot, a policy matter for discussion is likely to be the question of lunch. This may be a meal in a local pub or simply sandwiches eaten out on the ground, but the timing of it is worth consideration. Some shoots adopt the idea of having a short break for beer or soup at about 12.30 p.m. and then going straight on until about 2.30 or 3 p.m. They finish shooting then, have a late lunch, and those with a long way to motor home can make an early start. Big shooting lunches are all very well when everyone lives or is staying locally; but they are still rather a bore for the beaters, who have to hang around until the Guns appear again two or more hours after the previous drive. A short lunch break, or a longer one at the end of the day, also means that shooting can stop in good time to enable the birds to get up to roost before dark.

Another consideration for the close season is the well-being of the gundog. It needs more than just food and a walk now and then. Its mind should be kept active. If you can go pigeon shooting, that will be a help. But you should also take the dog for regular walks and sometimes carry two or three training dummies with you. Throw a dummy and walk on with the dog for a couple of hundred yards, then send the dog back. While it is exercising its memory, remembering where the first dummy fell, throw out another one. After it has delivered the first, the dog can then be sent on an unseen retrieve for the second. It is difficult to give a shooting dog sufficient exercise when it is not working, but it should certainly not be turned out loose to go and exercise itself. That nearly always leads to bad habits. Swimming is very good exercise, so if you are near a stretch of water take the dog for walks that way, and again have some dummies with you.

A dog's pads can become out of condition if most of its exercise is over soft ground, and so a certain amount of road work is advisable to keep them hard. Try to keep the dog's mind working. You need not teach it any parlour tricks, but you can send it to retrieve things while you are, for example, gardening. Send it for a glove that you left in the shed ten minutes ago; or chuck your old hat into a laurel bush while the dog is having a nap and then try a 'Hi, lost!' when it wakes up. Of course, if you have been in the habit of shooting marauding rabbits and squirrels in the garden, the dog may be disappointed at finding only a hat; but at least it will have used its mind to think about something more than when its next meal is going to appear.

Some men become absorbed in one sport to the exclusion of all others: sad in the summer when there is no fox-hunting, or lost in the winter when trout fishing has stopped. It is better, however, to be able to enjoy more than one sport, even though there is probably insufficient time to follow different interests which have the same season. Two that are reasonably complementary are shooting and game fishing, where the main season for one begins at about the time the other ends.

Game fishing is not just an earnest and serious affair, carried on by old gentlemen in funny hats who creep about and speak in whispers. It is a most satisfying sport and it takes one to beautiful parts of the country. But it is not easy, especially to start with : one useful piece of advice given by that old humbug, Izaak Walton, was that anglers should be patient 'and forbear swearing lest they be heard, and catch no fish'.

It is still possible to learn more about shooting even in the close season: the recognition of different birds, for instance, and their flying characteristics. If you go for a walk by a river or by a quiet part of the seashore, you can watch duck and snipe and waders with the eye of a shooter as well as a naturalist. Try to judge the range as a bird flies past; and when you imagine yourself shooting it, fix your eyes on its head only. Practise reading the flight path, especially when a bird gets up nearby. You will soon realise that there is nearly always plenty of time to take a controlled shot instead of immediately hurrying into an ill-judged one.

There is so much to learn about the many parts which go to make up the whole of shotgun shooting. Reading about it can help, which is the object of this book, but you also have to go out and *see* and *do* if you are going to benefit.

We hope that these chapters have informed the beginner and stirred old hands into investigating some of the wider aspects of their sport. And heeding the remarks of a Mr. Markland who, in 1727, wrote a poem on *The Art of Shooting Flying*. In a prologue, he said:

'I am sensible there is no becoming Sportsmen by Book. You may here find the Rules and proper Direction for that End; but Practice alone can make you Masters.'

NOTES ON THE PROOF OF SHOTGUNS AND OTHER SMALL ARMS

1. This is a guide published in 1960 by the authorities of the two proof houses, the Guardians of the Birmingham Proof House and the Gunmakers Company of London. Addresses:

The Proof House, Banbury Street, Birmingham, 5.

The Proof House, 48 Commercial Road, London, E.1.

2. Extracts are as follows:

'The present law on the subject is to be found in the Gun Barrel Proof Acts of 1868 and 1950 . . .'

'The Proof Acts lay down that no small arm may be sold . . . unless and until it has been fully proved and duly marked. The maximum penalty for such offences is £20 per barrel.'

'Arms previously proved . . . are deemed unproved if the barrels have been enlarged in the bore beyond certain defined limits, or if the barrel or action has been materially weakened in other respect . . .'

'The offence in dealing in unproved arms is committed by the seller, not by an unwitting purchaser.'

3. A Memorandum issued by the Gun Trade Association on re-proofing shotguns contains these points:

(a) Proof is the testing required by law of a new shotgun

[199]

(or other small arm) before sale, to ensure, as far as practicable, that it has adequate strength to stand up to the pressures and strains to which it will be exposed in use. Re-proof is the similar testing of a gun which has previously been proved. Both Proof and Re-proof of shotguns involve pressures some 70% higher than the service pressure. For example, in a 12-bore game gun the service pressure is taken to be 3 tons (6720 lbs.) per square inch. The need for strength is evident.

(b) If mishandled or neglected a gun may be weakened during even a short period of service so that, although it is marked as having been duly proved, it may have become out of Proof. Reliance on the Proof marks alone is therefore not sufficient. Early indications of weakness are often only apparent to those who have been trained to recognise them. Accordingly, inspection of guns by a Gunmaker at regular intervals is recommended and advice to submit for Re-proof should be followed without delay, to avoid undue risk of personal injury. If such advice is ignored the Gunmaker may reasonably refuse to repair or work on a gun.

(c) The main reasons which call for Re-proof are:
    (i) Indications of weakness in action or barrel, including cracks, pitting, bulges, or dents, and failure of the brazing of the lump.
    (ii) Potential weakening, such as by conversion to ejector, repair of the action or barrel by welding, electrolytic deposit of hard chrome or other metal in the barrel.
    (iii) Enlargement of the internal diameter of the barrel, or lengthening of the chamber, so that it no longer conforms with the existing Proof marks.

(iv) Replacement of action, barrel, barrel lug or extension.

(v) Fitting of any attachment, such as a variable choke, which must withstand the pressure of firing.

(vi) Black powder guns, even if still legally proved, should be re-proved to determine whether they are safe for use with modern cartridges.

(d) Guns will not be accepted for Re-proof unless their condition conforms to the requirements of the Rules of Proof. Although guns may be submitted by their owners direct to the Proof Houses, it is preferable that they be dealt with by a Gunmaker who knows the requirements and is able to do any preparatory work necessary. Guns are submitted at the owner's risk of failure and the Gunmaker is entitled to payment for his services regardless of the result.

(e) A gun which passes proof will be duly marked and may be used with confidence. In the event of rejection the Proof Authorities will deface the existing Proof Marks on the faulty part or parts. If the owner does not have these replaced the gun should be rendered completely unserviceable to prevent use by a person unaware of its unproved condition.

(f) Under the Gun Barrel Proof Act 1868, it is an offence, subject to a penalty not exceeding £20 per barrel, to sell, exchange, pawn or export a gun which has not passed Proof or Re-proof or has become unproved for any other reason.

4. Note that the Gun Barrel Proof Act 1978 increased the penalties above, para 2 and 3(f), from £20 per barrel to £1000 per offence.

THE PROOF OF GUNS FOR MAGNUM CARTRIDGES

1. A Memorandum issued by the Worshipful Company of Gunmakers of London and the Guardians of the Birmingham Proof House, 4th December, 1967.

Since the introduction in August, 1967, of Eley Magnum cartridges, the 12-bore $2\frac{3}{4}$-inch loaded with $1\frac{1}{2}$ oz. of shot and the 12-bore 3-inch loaded with $1\frac{5}{8}$ oz. shot, the Proof Houses, I.M.I. and the Gun Trade have received a number of enquiries from the shooting public as to whether these cartridges may safely be used in British or Foreign proved guns of the appropriate chamber length without special or magnum proof. I.M.I. publicity and the markings on cartridge cartons make clear that English guns using these Magnum cartridges must be specially proved to cover a maximum service pressure of $3\frac{1}{2}$ tons per square inch in lieu of the standard $3\frac{1}{4}$ tons for the 12-bore $2\frac{3}{4}$-inch chamber and 4 tons in lieu of $3\frac{1}{2}$ tons for the 12-bore 3-inch chamber. (The $2\frac{3}{4}$-inch Magnum $1\frac{1}{2}$ oz. load may, however, be used in standard proved 3-inch guns without additional proof.)

For over 40 years Special proof for heavy loads has been available at the London and Birmingham Proof Houses. Guns may be submitted on request to Magnum proof to cover these higher pressure levels. Proof Pressure

[202]

is between 60% and 80% in excess of declared maximum service pressure.

The present reciprocal recognition of the proof marks of seven European countries is not based on exact duplication of pressure levels or methods of proof or standards of view, but it is and has been accepted for many years, both in Great Britain and abroad that the various proofs are equivalent, gauge for gauge and chamber length for chamber length. One vital difference is that British guns proved since February 1955 have been marked with the highest mean or maximum service pressure in tons per square inch, while continental proved guns are marked with the actual proof pressure in kilograms per square centimetre, if they bear a pressure marking at all.

Other differences between European and British proof are to be found not only in the proof powders and loads used, but also in the methods of pressure measurement.

The European Proof Houses measure pressure with small copper crushers on pistons at 17 mm. and 162 mm. from the breech. Results are given in kgs. per square centimetre. Britain uses lead crushers on pistons at 1-inch and 6-inch. This method produces answers in tons per square inch. Results are not directly comparable on a mathematical scale.

Proof Houses in Europe have for some years proved guns on request for special loads. Guns intended for American markets are submitted in Belgium to a special proof 'Epreuve Superieure' and corresponding Special proofs in other countries.

In these circumstances, the Proof Houses of London and Birmingham recommend that 12-bore foreign shot-

[203]

guns of 2¾-inch and 3-inch chambers should not be used with magnum cartridges unless they have been proved and marked to a level of 1200 kgs. or are submitted to British Magnum Proof. In the case of Belgian guns, the special 'Epreuve Superieure' mark of the Liege Proof House denotes Magnum proof to the 1200 kgs. level. (12-bore 2¾-inch cartridge may, however, be used in standard 3-inch chambered guns marked to a proof level of 1000 kgs.)

Where no Proof Certificate is available or doubts exist as to proof marks, or as to the suitability of a gun to be used with or proved for Magnum cartridges, the advice of an experienced gunsmith or gunmaker should be sought. Some guns may withstand Magnum proof but be unsuitable for Magnum cartridges by reason of their light construction and consequent heavy recoil.

2. Further Statement on the Proof of Guns for Magnum Cartridges. To be read in conjunction with the Memorandum of 4th December, 1967, issued by the joint Proof Authorities.

In the Memorandum of December, 1967, the Proof Authorities recommended that Magnum cartridges should only be used in Foreign guns which have been proved to the continental Magnum Proof level of 1200 kg., or which have passed British Magnum Proof.

Since then, further tests of British and Belgian Proof cartridges and of Eley Magnum 2¾-inch and 3-inch cartridges have been carried out both in this country by British and Continental pressure methods and also in Liege, Belgium, the home of the Secretariat of the

International Proof Commission. All those European countries with which the United Kingdom has agreements for reciprocal recognition of proof marks work to Proof rules approved by the International Proof Commission or C.I.P.

These tests confirm that gun-barrel proof pressures in this country and in Belgium are on a par (though each has its advantages and limitations) but because of variations between British and Continental Proof as to the uplift from maximum cartridge service pressure to minimum proof pressure, Eley Magnum cartridges may be used in foreign guns bearing acceptable proof marks (12 × 2¾-inch proved at 900 kg. and 12 × 3-inch proved at 1000 kg.) without the need for special magnum proof. European Proof regulations provide that standard cartridges of 12 × 2¾-inch shall not exceed a pressure of 600 kg. per square centimetre, that is 3·82 tons. British regulations require that the maximum service pressure of 12 × 2¾-inch cartridges shall not exceed 3·25 tons – 510 kg. It is arguable that this lower level of the maximum service pressure allowed for cartridges offers a longer barrel life, less strain upon the gun and a higher margin of safe strength.

The British Proof Authorities accept that Continental guns proved to a similar proof pressure to that given British guns, may be used with higher pressure cartridges, but can accept no responsibility whatever for the result. They repeat their earlier advice that where doubt exists as to the suitability of a gun for Eley Magnum cartridges, the advice of the gun supplier or a reputable gunsmith should be sought.

It should be appreciated that these notes apply only to

Eley Magnum or other cartridges which carry an indication on their carton as to their pressure level and not to other Magnums about which no reliable information is available – some of which have been found to give excessive pressures.

NOTES ON THE PURCHASE OF
SECOND-HAND SHOTGUNS

Issued by the Guardians of the Birmingham Proof House

The purchase of a second-hand shotgun involves some-what similar risks to those incurred in buying a second-hand motor car, or an expensive second-hand watch. Each to a degree is the product of skilled craftsmen and in none is it a simple matter for the layman to detect every defect or weak-ness. To suggest that one should go to a reputable gunmaker or gunsmith and buy the best gun one can afford may be sound advice, but it is cold comfort to those who really can-not afford a good second-hand gun or to those who may be tempted to purchase a second-hand gun from an acquaint-ance, in the market place, at an auction or sale room or at the local tavern. A few words of advice on the subject may be timely.

When contemplating the purchase or sale of a used gun, check must be made that the proof marks remain valid. Proof marks indicate the soundness of the gun when it was last proved, but the gun may have been so altered that it is unproved at law although the proof marks remain.

The incidence of purchase tax on new guns, added to their already high cost, placed a premium on the better class of second-hand gun, so that there are many old guns being offered for sale which in more normal times would have been considered past further service. Where purchase is contemplated from sources other than reputable gunmakers, gunsmiths or dealers, it is suggested that the gun be submitted to a reputable gunmaker for a report on its condition prior to completion of the deal. Where difficulty is experienced in obtaining such a report, request may be made to one of the Proof Houses for advice as to whether the gun is or is not in fully proved condition. The Proof Houses should not be expected to advise as to mechanical condition, quality, or value.

A report of this nature is suggested and may be invaluable because a gun may have a number of faults not apparent to the inexpert eye.

An expert examination of the gun should determine:

1. Whether the gun has been nitro proved, bears the relative proof marks and is suitable for use with modern cartridges.

2. Whether the bores have been enlarged since the barrels were last proved.

3. Whether the barrels are in good condition generally; that is, free from rust, pitting, dents and bulges.

4. Whether the chambers have been altered to accept a longer case since the gun was last proved.

5. Whether the action is 'off the face' of the barrels, or otherwise loose.

6. Whether the action is in good, safe working order.

7. Whether the gun patterns well at normal distances. This is not a matter affecting the safety of the gun or its state in proof, but is of importance to the prospective purchaser.

It is regrettably true there are guns offered for sale by irresponsible persons which would not pass examination satisfactorily on any one of the several points enumerated above. Such a gun may well be unproved, unsafe, and fit only for use as a wall ornament.

The shooting public are given protection by the Gun Barrel Proof Acts of 1868 and 1950 under which it is an offence to offer for sale an unproved arm. Every shotgun must pass the proof test and bear proof marks, and where certain alterations have been effected since proof such as the opening out of the bore beyond defined limits to remove pitting, or the deepening of the chambers, the proof marks are rendered invalid, the gun becomes an unproved weapon, and must be submitted to a further proof test prior to sale.

The Proof Authorities and the Proof Houses were established for public security and one of their more important functions under the Proof Acts is to institute proceedings against offenders where the necessary evidence is put before them and is considered to justify such action. Proceedings have been instituted by one or other of the Proof Authorities on a number of occasions in recent years and in each case a substantial fine has been imposed. The offence in dealing in unproved arms is committed by the seller not by the purchaser.

Closer co-operation between the shooting public, gunmakers, and the Proof Authorities must result in a reduction of the risks involved in the purchase of second-hand shotguns from chance acquaintance, unscrupulous dealers, or misinformed friends.

ORGANISATIONS AND PUBLICATIONS CONCERNED WITH SHOOTING

1. British Field Sports Society: Director, Maj. Gen. J. M. Brockbank, 59 Kennington Road, London, S.E.1.
Works for the furtherance of all field sports, particularly combating propaganda issued by organisations opposed to them. Also issues excellent explanatory pamphlets for young people and can inform members where sport may be obtained.

2. Clay Pigeon Shooting Association: Secretary, A. P. Page, 107 Epping New Road, Buckhurst Hill, Essex.
Controls clay shooting throughout Great Britain and organises national championships. Can supply information about local clubs, most of which are affiliated to it.

3. The Game Conservancy: Secretary, Col. D. Bayne-Jardine, Fordingbridge, Hants.
Formed in 1969 by the merger between the Game Research Association and the Eley Game Advisory Station. Carries out scientific research and practical investigations into factors influencing the survival and numbers of game in the British Isles. Provides an advisory and information service on game production and management. Produces a range of advisory booklets and instructional film.

4. **Wildfowlers Association of Great Britain and Ireland:**
Director, Lt.-Cdr. J. W. Anderton, Marford Mill,
Rossett, Clwyd.
'W.A.G.B.I.' assists wildfowlers and rough shooters, protects their rights and organises rearing and ringing of
wildfowl. Many local gun clubs, even inland ones not
concerned with 'fowling, are affiliated to it. Help is given
to members seeking information about shooting areas,
especially where the foreshore rights belong to a local
club.

5. *The Field*, Carmelite House, Carmelite Street, London
E.C.4.
Articles on most sports, including shooting. Useful
advertisements for guns, dogs, shoots, etc.

6. *Shooting Times and Country Magazine*, 10 Sheet Street,
Windsor, Berks.
Articles and reports on game shooting and clay shooting.
The official organ of W.A.G.B.I., and carries news of
B.F.S.S. and C.P.S.A.

7. *The Gun Code*
Notes on safety, licences, proofing, game seasons, etc.
Should be read by every shooter when he gets his first
gun. Available from B.F.S.S.

8. *Eley Shotgun Cartridges for Game and Wildfowl Shooting* Describes cartridges, loads, shot sizes available, etc.
From Eley, P.O. Box 216, Witton, Birmingham.

A SUMMARY OF THE LAW RELATING TO THE POSSESSION AND USE OF FIREARMS AND AMMUNITION

The law relating to the purchase, possession and use of firearms and ammunition is contained in the Firearms Act, 1968 (hereinafter referred to as the Act).

This summary is divided according to the main classes of firearms, and, as the restrictions apply in different degrees at different ages, is sub-divided into age groups. Where necessary, restrictions are listed under more than one sub-heading.

A. Air weapons and ammunition, excluding any type declared by the Secretary of State to be specially dangerous.
  I. A person aged 17 and over – no restrictions.
  II. A person aged under 17 but not under 14
      (a) MAY NOT purchase or hire any air weapon or ammunition:
      (b) MAY be made a gift of or borrow an air weapon or ammunition:
      (c) MAY NOT be in possession of an air weapon in a public place except
          (i) an air gun or air rifle which is so covered with a securely fastened gun cover that it cannot be fired; or

[212]

    (ii) as a member of an approved club while engaged as such a member in or in connection with target practice; or

    (iii) while using the weapon or ammunition at a shooting gallery where the only firearms used are either air weapons or miniature rifles not exceeding ·23 calibre.

(d) MAY use an air weapon without supervision.

III. A person aged under 14

  (a) MAY NOT purchase or hire any air weapon or ammunition:

  (b) MAY NOT be made a gift of any air weapon or ammunition:

  (c) MAY NOT be in possession of an air weapon or ammunition except

    (i) while under the supervision of a person of or over the age of 21 (the air weapon must not be discharged in such a manner that the missile will pass beyond the premises upon which the shooting is taking place); or

    (ii) as a member of an approved club while engaged as such a member in or in connection with target practice; or

    (iii) while using the weapon or ammunition at a shooting gallery where the only firearms used are either air weapons or miniature rifles not exceeding ·23 calibre.

Note: It is an offence to make a gift of an air weapon or ammunition for an air weapon to any person under the age of 14, or part with the possession of an air weapon or ammunition for it to a person under that age except as detailed in III (c) above.

B. Shotguns with barrels of twenty-four inches or more in length, and ammunition for them.

  I. A person aged 17 and over

    (a) MAY NOT purchase, acquire or have in his possession a shotgun without first being in possession of a shotgun certificate unless

      (i) he is covered by the special exemptions contained in sections 7–15 inclusive of the Act; these include registered firearms dealers, auctioneers, carriers or warehousemen, slaughterers; the possession in stated cases of signalling apparatus; during theatrical performances; in the production of a cinematograph film; the carrying of a firearm or ammunition belonging to another person holding a certificate and for the use of that person for sporting purposes only; the use by members of rifle clubs or cadet forces while engaged in drill or target practice; the use on miniature rifle ranges or shooting galleries; for starting race meetings; where a permit has been obtained from the chief officer of police in accordance with the terms of the permit; or

      (ii) he is covered by the exemption for certain Crown servants contained in section 54 of the Act; or

      (iii) he is using a shotgun at a place approved for shooting at artificial targets by the chief officer of police for the area in which the place is situated; or

      (iv) he is borrowing a shotgun from the occupier of private premises for use on those premises in the presence of the occupier; or

[214]

    (v) he holds a firearm certificate issued in Northern Ireland authorising him to possess a shotgun; or

    (vi) he has been in Great Britain for not more than 30 days in all in the preceding twelve months.

Note: A shotgun certificate is not need to purchase, acquire or have in one's possession cartridges for use in a shotgun.

II. A person aged under 17 but not under 15

    (a) MAY NOT purchase or hire a shotgun or ammunition:

    (b) MAY be made a gift of or borrow a shotgun or ammunition provided he has first obtained a shotgun certificate, unless exempted from this requirement as mentioned above:

    (c) MAY use it without supervision.

III. A person aged under 15

    (a) MAY NOT purchase or hire any shotgun or ammunition:

    (b) MAY NOT be made a gift of a shotgun or ammunition:

    (c) MAY NOT have in his possession an assembled shotgun unless he is also in possession of a shotgun certificate (unless exempted from the requirement as mentioned above) and

        (i) is supervised by a person of or over the age of 21; or

        (ii) the shotgun is so covered with a securely fastened gun cover that it cannot be fired.

Note: It is an offence to make a gift of any shotgun or ammunition for a shotgun to any person under the age of 15.

C. Firearms and ammunition other than air weapons and shotguns and ammunition for them but including smooth bore guns having a barrel length of less than 24 inches and air weapons of a type declared to be specially dangerous.

I. A person aged 17 and over

    (a) MAY NOT purchase, acquire or have in his possession any such firearm without first being in possession of a valid firearm certificate, unless covered by the exemptions in the Act as set out in B. I (a) (i) and (ii) above.

II. A person aged under 17 but not under 14

    (a) MAY NOT purchase or hire any such firearm or ammunition.

    (b) MAY be made a gift of any such firearm or ammunition providing he is in possession of a valid firearm certificate.

    (c) MAY have any such firearm in his possession without a firearm certificate if covered by the exemptions as mentioned above.

III. A person aged under 14

    (a) MAY NOT purchase or acquire any such firearm or ammunition.

    (b) MAY NOT be made a gift of or borrow any such firearm or ammunition.

    (c) MAY NOT have in his possession any such firearm or ammunition; except

        (i) as a member of a rifle club or miniature rifle club or cadet corps approved by the Secretary of State, when engaged as such a member in, or in connection with, drill or target practice; or

        (ii) at a miniature rifle range or shooting gallery

at which no firearms are used other than miniature rifles not exceeding ·23 calibre; or

(iii) when carrying a firearm or ammunition belonging to another person holding a certificate, under instructions from and for the use of that other person for sporting purposes only.

Note: It is an offence to make a gift of any such firearm or ammunition to a person under the age of 14, or part with the possession of such firearm or ammunition to a person under that age, except as set out in C. III (c) above.

D. Prohibited weapons and ammunition.

Except with the authority of the Defence Council, it is unlawful to purchase, acquire, or have in one's possession

(a) any firearm which is so designed or adapted that, if pressure is applied to the trigger, missiles continue to be discharged until the pressure is removed from the trigger or the magazine containing the missiles is empty; or

(b) any weapon of whatever description designed or adapted for the discharge of any noxious liquid, gas or other thing; or

(c) any ammunition containing, or designed or adapted to contain, any such noxious thing.

SHOTGUN CERTIFICATES AND GAME LICENCES

1. Gun licences have been abolished. Since May, 1968, Shotgun Certificates have taken their place.
2. In order to possess a shotgun, a certificate must be obtained from the police, who provide the application form. The certificate costs £7 and is valid for three years.
3. A game licence is required to shoot game (see notes to Appendix G). The licence costs £6 and lasts from August 1st until July 31st the following year. A shortened period from August to 31st October or from November to 31st July costs £4. For any consecutive fourteen days the fee is £2. A gamekeeper's licence costs £4 for a year.
4. Game may not be shot on Sundays or on Christmas Day.

NOTES ON THE PROTECTION OF BIRDS ACTS, 1954 AND 1967

1. Game Birds Excluded. The Acts do not apply to game birds which are listed as follows: Pheasant, partridge, grouse, blackgame and, in Scotland, ptarmigan. The Game Act of 1831 caters for game birds.
2. General Protection. All wild birds are protected unless named in the Acts in the list of birds which may be shot; the Acts prescribe the period of the shooting season for each bird in that list. The shooting seasons are, with the exception of the season for woodcock, applicable in all counties of England, Scotland and Wales.
3. Shooting on Sundays and on Christmas Day. The Acts prohibit the shooting of any wild bird in Scotland on Sundays and on Christmas Day. Regarding England and Wales, there is no such prohibition but the Acts give power to the Home Secretary to prohibit shooting on Sundays in any county. If in doubt as to the position in your county, ask your local council or police.
4. Decoys. It is an offence under the Acts to use as a decoy any live bird which is tethered or which is secured by means of braces or other similar appliances, or which is blind, maimed or injured.
5. Use of Boats. The Acts make it illegal to use 'any mechanically propelled vehicle, boat or any aircraft in

immediate pursuit of a wild bird for the purpose of driving, killing or taking that bird'.

6. List of Birds which may be Shot and the Respective Shooting Seasons.

1st October–31st January	12th August–31st January
Capercaillie	Jack Snipe
	Common Snipe

Inland – 1st September–31st January
Foreshore – 1st September–20th February
(Foreshore is defined in the Acts as 'in or over any area below high water mark of ordinary spring tides')

Common Pochard	Pintail	Wild geese –
Common Scoter	Scaup-duck	Bean
Gadwall	Shoveler	Canada
Garganey Teal	Teal	Greylag
Goldeneye	Tufted duck	Pinkfoot
Long-tailed duck	Velvet Scoter	Whitefront
Mallard	Wigeon	

1st September–31st January

Coot	Golden Plover
Common Redshank	Grey Plover
Curlew (other than Stone curlew)	Moorhen
Bar-tailed Godwit	Whimbrel

In Scotland: 1st September–31st January ⎫
In England and Wales: 1st Oct.–31st Jan. ⎭ Woodcock

7. List of Birds which may be Shot at any Time of the Year by an Authorised Person.

Cormorant	Magpie
Carrion Crow	Red-breasted Merganser
Domestic Pigeon gone feral	(in Scotland only)

[220]

Hooded Crow
House-sparrow
Goosander (in Scotland only)
Greater Black-backed Gull
Lesser Black-backed Gull
Herring Gull
Jackdaw
Jay
Rock-dove (in Scotland only)
Rook
Shag
Starling
Stock-dove
Wood-pigeon
Collared Dove

Note:

(a) Under the Acts an 'authorised person' is the landowner, tenant or person having the sporting rights, or a person having permission from one of these three; or any person authorised in writing by the Local Authority or by certain statutory bodies such as the Nature Conservancy, River Boards and local Fishery Committees.

(b) The shooting seasons for game birds, which may only be shot by holders of a Game Licence, are as follows, both days inclusive:

Pheasant – 1st October to 1st February
Partridge – 1st September to 1st February
Grouse – 12th August to 10th December
Blackgame – 20th August to 10th December
Ptarmigan – 12th August to 10th December

Copies of the Acts may be obtained from H.M. Stationery Office or through most booksellers.

(c) A Game Licence is required before shooting snipe and woodcock, and also hares.

(d) Amendments are continually being made to these Acts by which species are moved from one Schedule to another. For example, oystercatchers and bullfinches may now be shot in certain areas. Also, bird sanctuaries are defined and orders are made prohibiting Sunday shooting in certain counties.

[221]

CLEANING A SHOTGUN

1. Have two cleaning rods, one for the cleaning rag or brush and one for the oily mop used for finally oiling the barrels after cleaning.
2. Push small bits of rolled-up newspaper through the barrels in the first place, thus removing the main dirt and prolonging the life of the cleaning rag.
3. Instead of using ordinary rag or tow for cleaning the barrels, try the special Shotgun Patches made by Parker Hale. These are made the right size according to bore and so save time.
4. Have a phosphor-bronze brush for stubborn bits of fouling.
5. Use a rust-preventing oil, such as Young's ·303 cleaner, for the inside of the barrels and a lighter oil, like Three-in-One, for the working parts.
6. Use a feather – the quill for cleaning round and under the extractors, and the soft end for lightly oiling the triggers, base of the rib, etc. A fairly stiff feather such as that from a pigeon's tail is better than a soft one like a pheasant's.
7. If the gun is very wet after rain, stand it on its muzzles to drain the water away down the barrels and not back into the action. Use blotting paper for drying such places as the base of the rib where it joins the barrels. Examine the gun the day after cleaning to see if there is any

sweating, which will need wiping and re-oiling. After a wet day, the locks of a side-lock gun can be removed, or the bottom plate of a boxlock, and water mopped out with a clean cotton rag. The screwdriver must fit the screw heads accurately, which probably means that it will need filing in order to enter the fine slots. Many gun-smiths, incidentally, consider that unskilled owners would do less harm to their guns if they did *not* attempt to take them to bits.

8. The stock should be wiped clean of mud and have a little linseed oil rubbed in as a preservative. For a better shine, use 'artist's quality' linseed oil mixed with about a third as much of the same quality turpentine. Do not cover the wood with gun-oil, which can cause it to swell and interfere with the working of the lock, making it unsafe. Dents and scratches can be dealt with by applying wet felt and pressing on it with a hot iron: the steam forced into the wood raises the mark.

BIBLIOGRAPHY

B.B., *The Shooting Man's Bedside Book*, Eyre & Spottiswoode, 1948

Brander, Michael, *Rough Shooter's Dog*, Gentry Books, 1971

Burrard, Sir Gerald, *In the Gunroom*, Herbert Jenkins, 1951

Burrard, Sir Gerald, *The Modern Shotgun, Vol I: The Gun, Vol II: The Cartridge, Vol III: The Gun and the Cartridge*, Herbert Jenkins 1955–1959

Coats, Archie, *Pigeon Shooting*, André Deutsch, 2nd revised edition, 1970

Coats, Archie, *Amateur Keeper*, Studio Vista, 1962

Duncan, S. and Thorne, G., *The Complete Wildfowler*, Herbert Jenkins, 1950

Educational Productions, *Shotgun Shooting*, Know the Game Series, 1963

Erlandson, Keith, *Gundog Training*, Barrie & Jenkins, 1979

Garwood, G. T., *Gough Thomas's Gun Book*, Black, 1969

Gladstone, H. S., *Record Bags and Shooting Records*, H. F. and G. Witherby, revised edition, 1930

Grattan, G. A. and Willett, R., *Rough Shooting*, Faber & Faber, 2nd revised edition, 1975

Hare, C. E., *The Language of Field Sports*, Country Life, revised edition, 1949

Harold, Robert, *The Age of Firearms*, Cassell, 1959

Harrison, Jeffrey G., *Wealth of Wildfowl*, Corgi, new edition, 1973

Hawker, Colonel Peter, *Instructions to Young Sportsmen*, Richmond Publishing Co., 2nd facsimile of 1833 edition, 1975

Jefferies, Richard, *The Gamekeeper at Home*, facsimile of 1879 edition, Tideline, 1973

Jefferies, Richard, *The Amateur Poacher*, facsimile of 1878 edition, Tideline, 1973

Johnson, C. E., *The Game Laws Simplified*, Police Review, 1964

Kemp, Michael, *A Shoot of Your Own*, A. & C. Black, 1978

Moxon, P. R. A., *Gundogs: Training and Field Trials*, Popular Dogs, 1973

Moxon, P. R. A., *Gundogs: Modern Training Methods*, Shooting Times Library, 1946

Moxon, P. R. A., *Training the Rough Shooter's Dog*, Popular Dogs, 1977

Parker, Eric, *The Shooting Week-end Book*, Seeley Service, no date

Payne Gallwcy, Sir R., *Shooting, 2 volumes*, Badminton Library, Longmans Green, 1886

Powell, Bill, *The Grey Geese Call*, Herbert Jenkins, 1956

Sedgwick, Noel M., *The Gun on Saltings and Stubble*, Herbert Jenkins, 1949

Sedgwick, Noel M., *Shooting Round the Year*, Herbert Jenkins, 1952

Sedgwick, Noel M., *Shooting Wildfowl and Game*, Herbert Jenkins, 1953

Sedgwick, Noel M., *With Dog and Gun*, Herbert Jenkins, 1951

Sedgwick, Noel M., *The Young Shot*, Black, 3rd revised

edition, 1975

Sedgwick, Noel M., Whitaker, Peter, and Harrison, Jeffrey, *The New Wildfowler in the 1970s*, Barrie & Jenkins, 2nd revised edition, 1970

Sharpe, R., *Dog Training by Amateurs*, Country Life, 1955

Shephard, Michael, *Come Wildfowling*, Museum Press, 1953

Stanbury, Percy and Carlisle, G. L., *Clay Pigeon Marksmanship*, Barrie & Jenkins, 3rd edition, 1974

Stanbury, Percy and Carlisle, G. L., *Shotgun Marksmanship*, Barrie & Jenkins, 4th edition, 1980

Standfield, F. G., *Syndicate Shooting*, Herbert Jenkins, 1961

Thomas, Gough, *Shotguns and Cartridges*, Black, 3rd revised edition, 1975

Waddington, Richard, *Grouse Shooting and Moor Management*, Faber & Faber, 1958

Willock, Colin, *Kenzie, the Wild Goose Man*, Deutsch, new impression, 1972

Willock, Colin, *The Gun-punt Adventure*, Faber & Faber, 1958